# THE PILGRIM BOOK
## OF BIBLE STORIES

# THE PILGRIM BOOK OF BIBLE STORIES

THE GREAT STORIES OF THE BIBLE
RETOLD IN A FRESH AND LIVELY WAY
FOR TODAY'S CHILDREN

*Illustrated by Diana Shimon*

THE
PILGRIM
PRESS
Cleveland

First published in USA and Canada by
The Pilgrim Press,
700 Prospect Avenue East, Cleveland, Ohio 44115
pilgrimpress.com

First published in English outside North America under the title *The New Illustrated Bible* by
John Hunt Publishing Ltd,
46a West Street, New Alresford, UK SO24 9AU

Copyright © 2003 John Hunt Publishing Ltd

Text © 2003 Mark Water

Illustrations © 2003 Diana Shimon

Designed by Andrew Milne Design, West Sussex, UK

07  06  05  04  03  02      5  4  3  2  1

A catalog record for this book is available from the Library of Congress and the British Library.

North America ISBN 0-8298-1487-6

English Language outside North America ISBN 1-84298-091-2

Typeset in Goudy by Andrew Milne Design

Printed by Times Publishing Group, Malaysia

# INTRODUCTION

The aim of The Pilgrim Book of Bible Stories *is to bring the Bible to life for young readers, aged 9-12. Though it covers all the usual Bible stories, with their drama and passion, it does much more than this. The balance of text approximates to the text of the Bible itself. So weight is given to the laws of Leviticus, the Song of Solomon, and many passages usually ignored. Wisdom literature, prophecy, vision and parable are given as much space as historical adventure. In terms of story and event Balaam and Balaak are covered as well as Joshua and Caleb, Jael and Barak as well as Gideon.*

*Divided into 19 chapters, each has an introduction that reveals the developing thread of the story, linking history to interpretation, literature to life. This approach roots the stories in the historical reality of their times.*

*The artwork is extensively researched, and indeed many of the pictures have been drawn by the Israeli artist in situ. Diana Shimon captures the bleakness of the desert, the beauty of the fields and olive groves, the tumble of village life, the work of the potters and smiths, the harsh Middle Eastern light. Side panels provide background information on artifacts and customs, writings and beliefs. Direct quotes from the Bible texts are illustrated and draw the reader into the world of the story tellers and their listeners. Bible references on each page relate the story to the main Bible text.*

*This is the most complete color children's Bible available, capturing the full story of the chosen people's 1,000 year plus experience of God, and ending with its spread to the rest of the world.*

# CONTENTS

## HEBREW SCRIPTURES

| Contents | Bible Characters | Period | Bible books | Page |
|---|---|---|---|---|

8

9

| Contents | Bible Characters | Period | Bible books | Page |
|---|---|---|---|---|

| Contents | Bible Characters | Period | Bible books | Page |
|---|---|---|---|---|

10

## CHAPTER 13 *Daniel with the lions*
From the Bible books of Ezekiel and Daniel **209**

## CHAPTER 14 *Jonah's fishy tale*
From the Bible books of Hosea, Amos, Micah, Jonah, Esther, Obediah, Habakkuk, Zechariah and Malachi **225**

13

# NEW TESTAMENT

14

16

# Hebrew Scriptures

## Chapter 1: From the Bible book of Genesis

# Noah and the Great Flood

## Introduction

*This book begins at the beginning, with God creating the whole world, including us humans — made to be just like God.*

*As well as beauty, there is drama and sadness in the garden of Eden that God created.*

*The first murder is not hushed up.*

*Then comes God's rescue of Noah, his family and thousands of creatures from a great flood.*

*The story of the world's first disastrous building project, the uncompleted tower of Babel, follows.*

*Abraham, a great person of faith, is introduced. Although Abraham is elderly and childless, God promises that he will found a great nation.*

*The story of Lot's wife being turned into a pillar of salt is also included, along with the story of Abraham's first son, Ishmael, child of Hagar.*

# In the beginning

CREATOR GOD

In the beginning, God made heaven and earth. God breathed a wind over the deep emptiness. God made the light and called it day.

God made the darkness and called it night.

God made water, and God made the sky.

God made the ground and all its trees and plants, as well as all the vegetables and fruits.

God made the sun and the moon, the twinkling stars, and the animals, birds, fish and insects.

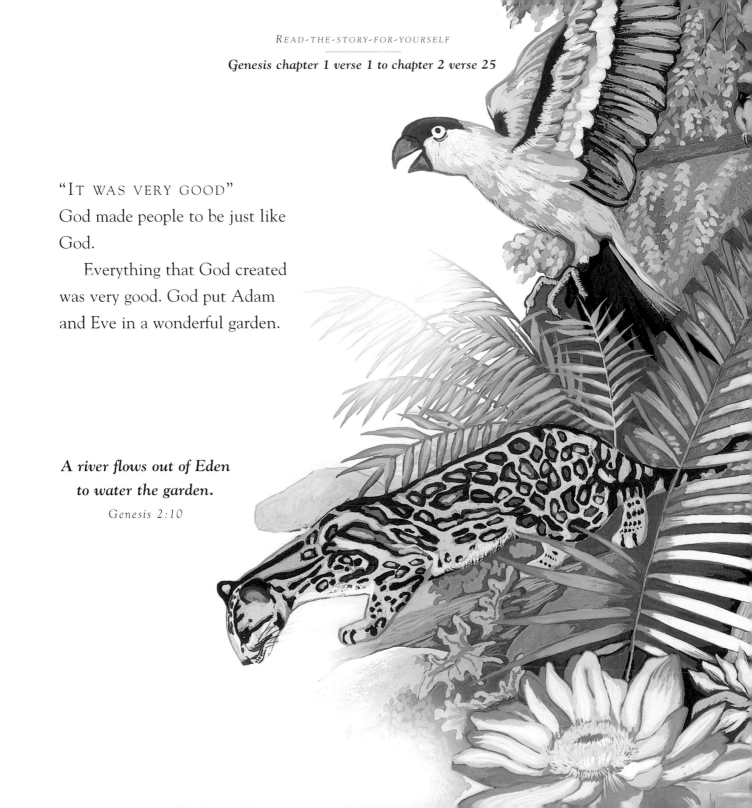

"IT WAS VERY GOOD"
God made people to be just like
God.

    Everything that God created
was very good. God put Adam
and Eve in a wonderful garden.

**A river flows out of Eden
to water the garden.**
*Genesis 2:10*

# The day the world changed

20 "So you can't eat the fruit on the trees?" murmured a snake to Eve.

"We can," Eve said. "But not the fruit on the tree giving knowledge of good and evil. God says if we eat that, we'll die."

"God's lying," hissed the snake. "You won't die. You'll be clever like God."

Eve ate the mouth-watering fruit and gave some to Adam.

It was true that the tree gave Adam and Eve knowledge. But God was angry at all of them. Adam and Eve had to leave the garden, but first, God made clothes for them.

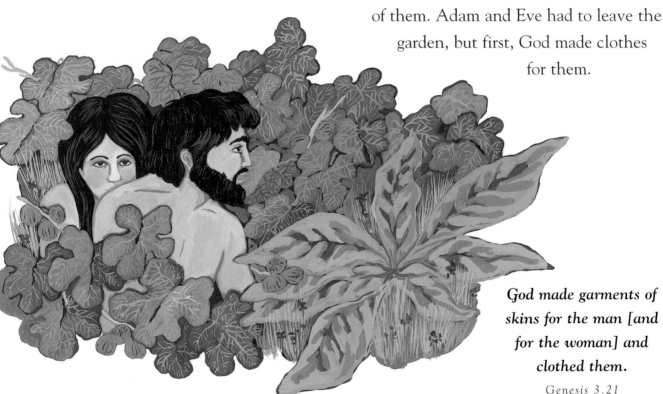

*God made garments of skins for the man [and for the woman] and clothed them.*

Genesis 3.21

## MURDER

"I can't stand him. I'll kill him."

Eve's eldest son, Cain, a farmer, was jealous of his brother Abel.

One day, Cain killed his brother and buried his body.

"Where's Abel?" asked God.

"Search me. Am I my brother's keeper?"

"Abel's blood fell on the ground," said God.

"Now nothing will grow for you."

So Cain had to leave.

He wandered far away from God.

21

*Cain rose up against his brother Abel and killed him.*

Genesis 4:8

# Rain into rainbow

### RAIN, RAIN, RAIN

God told Noah to build an ark. When the rains came, Noah and all his family went into the ark. With them, they took two of every creature on earth.

It seemed to rain for years.

Then it stopped.

Noah sent out a dove to see if the water had gone down. But the dove couldn't find any trees or ground to land on. It returned to the ark and landed on Noah's outstretched hand. Noah brought the dove into the ark.

**Flood warnings**

All over the world native peoples have passed down tales of a terrible flood. In one story the gods decided to drown the world because there was so much noise that they could not sleep. In another, the Epic of Gilgamesh, a man called Uta-Napishtim tells how the gods instructed him to build a boat to escape a flood. Like Noah, he sent out birds to check if the water had gone down.

Many scholars believe that the stories may be based on memories of an actual worldwide flood that took place at the end of the last Ice Age — the flood described in the Bible.

23

*The flood continued forty days on the earth . . . and bore up the ark, and it rose high above the earth.*

Genesis 7:17

24

[God said] "As long as
the earth endures,
seedtime and harvest,
cold and heat, summer
and winter, day and
night, shall not cease."

*Genesis 8:22*

A week later Noah sent off the dove again. The dove
flew back. It had a freshly picked olive leaf in its beak.
Yes — the floods were going down at last.

Noah waited another week and sent the dove out
again. It never came back.

"There must be dry land around," thought Noah.

## RAINBOW

"Come out of the ark now, Noah," God said.

So out they came — from the tiniest ant to the
largest elephant.

And, in the sky, a most magnificent rainbow
greeted them. "This rainbow is a sign of my promises

to you and to all the earth," God explained. All of Noah's family looked at the dazzling colors in the rainbow and knew that God loved them.

*Bring out with you every living thing . . . birds and animals and every creeping thing.*

Genesis 8:17

# The tower of Babel

> *"Come, let us build
> ourselves a city, and
> a tower."*
>
> *Genesis 11:4*

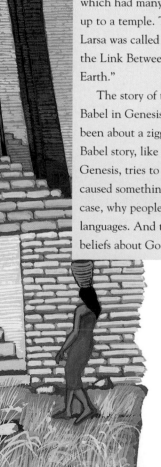

### Ziggurats

Cities in Mesopotamia often had a tower called a "ziggurat," which had many steps leading up to a temple. The ziggurat at Larsa was called "The House of the Link Between Heaven and Earth."

The story of the tower of Babel in Genesis may have been about a ziggurat. The Babel story, like others in Genesis, tries to explain what caused something — in this case, why people speak different languages. And the story shares beliefs about God.

## A TALL STORY

"Let's make a name for ourselves," said the people who lived by the Euphrates River.

"How?"

"We'll build a tower with a top that touches the sky. We'll be famous. No one will be able to put a stop to us or split us up."

## DANGEROUS TALK

God saw what they were doing. "If they carry on like this, they'll think they can do anything," God said.

So God muddled up their one language into a babble of different languages.

"Talk sense," each one said, "I can't understand a word you're saying."

Work on the tower stopped, and the people drifted away to live in other places.

28

# Into the unknown

*Abram took his wife
Sarai and his brother's
son Lot.*

Genesis 12:5

*Now there was a famine
in the land. So Abram
went down to Egypt.*

Genesis 12:10

Abraham lived in Haran, where everyone worshiped the moon. One day God said, "Leave this place, and go to the land I'll show you."

So Abraham set out, with his wife Sarah, and his nephew Lot.

They travelled hundreds of miles. At last, in the south of Canaan, God said, "You've arrived. Look around. I'm giving all this land to you and your descendants." And Abraham believed God.

*Genesis chapter 12 verses 1 to 20 and chapter 15 verses 1 to 6*

*Look toward heaven
and count the stars,
if you are able.*

Genesis 15:5

LIAR!
Famine! Abraham set
off again, through the
wilderness to Egypt.

Now Sarah was beautiful and
Abraham was scared. He said, "Some Egyptian will
murder me to marry you. Say you're my sister."

Pharaoh fell in love with Sarah. He gave Abraham sheep, cattle, camels, donkeys
and servants. Abraham took them all, and Pharaoh took Sarah. When Pharaoh
found out the truth he threw Abraham, Sarah and Lot out of the country. Egyptians
hated liars.

THE STARS
Back in Canaan, God spoke to Abraham. "Look at the stars. Count them if you can.
I'll give you as many descendants as there are stars." And Abraham believed God.

# A city in flames

30

Abraham's nephew Lot made a serious error. He went off to live in the city of Sodom, to the south of the Dead Sea.

Sodom was a vile, evil city.

One evening, Lot was sitting by the city gates when he saw two strangers. They were angels, but Lot didn't know that. He did know that it wasn't safe to be out in Sodom after dark.

"Come and stay at my house," Lot said.

That night the angels said, "This city will be destroyed. As soon as it's light, get away with your family. Run for your lives. And don't look back."

*Lot's wife behind him, looked back, and she became a pillar of salt.*

Genesis 19:26

As Lot was escaping with his wife and two daughters he heard a great roaring sound. The ground was shaking. There was a terrible smell.

Lot's wife couldn't stop herself. She turned round. The delay was fatal.

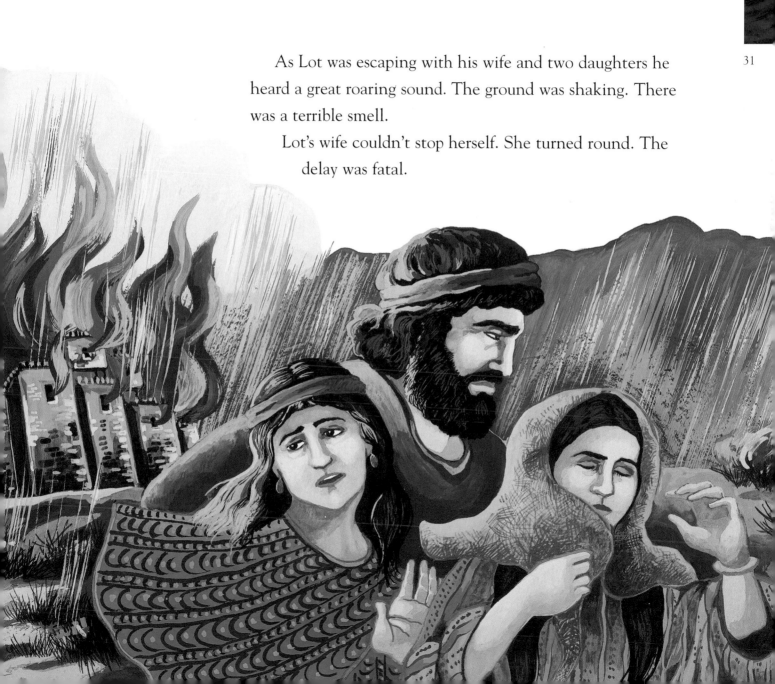

# Ismael is looked after

32

Ishmael was Abraham's first child. His pride and joy.

Ishmael's mother, Hagar, was a slave. She belonged to Sarah, who was Abraham's wife. Sarah was childless, so she gave Hagar to her husband as a second wife (that was the custom in those days).

Later, Sarah had a baby, Isaac.

"Spoilt brat!" thought Ishmael and made fun of Isaac.

"Throw that slave and her child out!" shouted Sarah.

"Do as Sarah says," God said.

Hagar and Ishmael wandered in the desert till their water was gone and they collapsed. Then Hagar heard a voice, an angel. "God has heard the boy crying," the angel said. He led them to a well.

God was with Ishmael and he grew up to be a great desert warrior.

> **Name Change**
> God changed Abram's name to Abraham and Sarai's name to Sarah (Genesis 17:5) as a sign of God's promises to them.

*So Abraham rose early in the morning, and took bread, and a skin of water, and gave it to Hagar.*

Genesis 21:14

# Abraham's amazing faith

INTRODUCTION

*This book starts with God ordering Abraham to sacrifice his much loved son, Isaac.*

*Abraham's servant is then sent on a seemingly impossible mission to find a girl, whose name and address he does not know. And the girl must be prepared to become Isaac's bride without even meeting him.*

*The story of God's love for God's people, the Israelites, then focuses on cheats.*

*Jacob cheats elder brother Esau out of his birthright.*

*Jacob is helped in all this by their scheming mother, Rebekah.*

*Then the cheat, Jacob, is outwitted by his ever-so-cunning uncle, Laban.*

*Yet through all this God promises to be with Jacob, to protect Jacob and to make a great nation of his descendants.*

# God's test for Abraham

34

### THE KNIFE IS POISED

Abraham was an old man when he and his wife, Sarah, had a child.

Now God told Abraham to take his son, Isaac, and sacrifice him!

Abraham cut the wood to burn the sacrifice. He gave the wood to Isaac to carry. Abraham had the fire and a very sharp knife.

Isaac asked his father the burning question: "I see the fire and the wood, but where is the lamb for the sacrifice?"

Abraham calmly replied, "God will provide the sacrifice, my son."

Then Abraham built an altar, arranged the wood on it, tied up Isaac, and put him on top of the wood. Abraham took a firm grip on his gleaming knife, raised his hand to . . .

## A RAM TO THE RESCUE

. . . when he heard a voice ringing in his ears.

It was God's angel calling him, "Abraham! Abraham!"

Abraham froze. "I'm here," he replied.

"Don't lay a finger on the boy," the angel instructed.

"I know for sure that you fear God, as you would have given God your only son."

Then Abraham looked up.

God had provided the sacrifice.

There, caught in a bush by his horns, was a ram.

Abraham then sacrificed the ram instead of Isaac.

*Isaac said to his father Abraham, "Father! . . . The fire and wood are here, but where is the lamb for a burnt offering?"*

Genesis 22:7

35

# A marriage made in heaven

36

### A BRIDE FOR ISAAC

Abraham was now very old. His thoughts turned to the future. What would happen to God's followers after his death?

Abraham's son, Isaac, needed a wife, but she had to be an Israelite. Abraham turned to his trusted head servant.

"Swear by God," Abraham ordered his servant, "the God of heaven and earth, that you will not take a wife for my son from the daughters of the Canaanites. Go to my country and my people and find a bride for Isaac there."

"But," ventured the servant, "what if this woman refuses to come back with me?"

"That won't happen," said Abraham confidently. "God will send an angel ahead of you."

### THE SERVANT PRAYED

So off the servant went, with ten of Abraham's camels laden with gifts. He arrived at a town called Nahor and his thirsty camels eyed the well, longingly.

The servant prayed: "God, may I be successful today. Please show your great love to Abraham in this way."

### THE WATER TEST FOR REBEKAH

The servant prayed that if the girl who gave him water to drink also offered to water his camels, then she should be Isaac's bride.

**Before he had finished
speaking, there was
Rebekah . . . coming out
with her water jar on
her shoulder.**

Genesis 24:15

# A successful mission

38

### CAMELS WATERED

"Here is a drink for you, sir," said Rebekah politely to the servant. Then she emptied her water jar into a trough for his ten camels.

That was it. Rebekah was the one. "Thank God for guiding me in this way," the servant prayed.

The servant then gave Rebekah a gold ring and two gold bracelets. He asked about her father, and if he could stay the night with her family.

### LABAN'S WELCOME

Rebekah ran back home. She had so much to tell her mom, her dad Bethuel, and Laban, her brother. When Laban saw the ring and the bracelets, he ran out to the well.

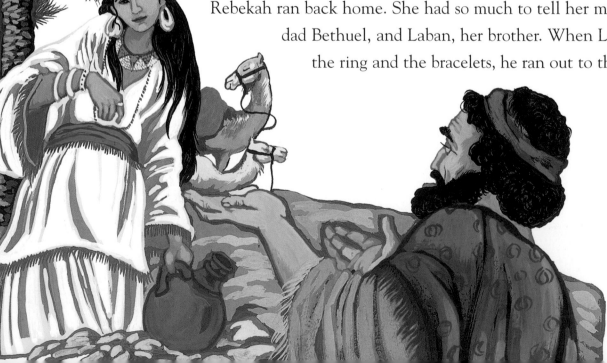

"Come and stay with me," Laban said to Abraham's servant. "You're very welcome." Laban looked after the camels, giving them straw and water.

### "REBEKAH IS YOURS"

Bethuel and Laban listened intently to the servant's story. They agreed to his wish.

"This is clearly from God," Bethuel and Laban concluded. "Rebekah is yours. Take her and return to Abraham. As God has said, Rebekah must marry your master's son."

So Rebekah returned with Abraham's servant. She met Isaac, who fell in love with her, and became his wife.

**When she had finished giving him a drink, she said, "I will draw for your camels also."**

*Genesis 24:19*

### One happy family

The amazing thing about this story is that Abraham's servant went straight to the home of a family who were already related to Abraham.

Rebekah was the daughter of Bethuel.

Bethuel was the son of Milcah and Nahor.

Nahor was Abraham's brother.

So when Abraham's son, Isaac, married Rebekah, he was marrying his father's great-niece.

For Rebekah was the grand-daughter of Abraham's brother.

*Rebekah's family tree*

```
Abraham ————————— Nahor
   |                 |
 Isaac            Bethuel
                     |
                  Rebekah
```

# Nonidentical twins

40

### ESAU AND JACOB

Isaac and Rebekah had twin sons.

The first-born son was Esau and the second-born son was Jacob. But nobody would have guessed that they were twins.

Esau loved the open fields. He became a skilled hunter.

But Jacob was quieter — more of a stay-at-home type.

### A BOWL OF SOUP

Jacob was jealous of Esau because he was the oldest.

One day Esau came home famished after hunting in the fields. His mouth watered as he smelled the lentil soup Jacob was stirring.

"I'm starving," announced Esau. "Let me have some of your soup."

"OK," said cunning Jacob, "but only in exchange for your rights as the firstborn son."

"OK, it's a deal. Just give me some of your red soup," responded Esau.

## Esau gives away his birthright

*The firstborn son*
In those days, the first born son inherited twice as much from his father as the second son did. This was the "birthright" Esau traded away.

*The blessing*
In those days, people believed that a blessing released a power that could never be undone. Isaac couldn't take back the blessing that Jacob stole. This blessing would make Jacob the head of his people.

*Once when Jacob was cooking a stew, Esau came in from the field . . . Esau said to Jacob, "Let me eat some of that red stuff, for I am famished!"*

Genesis 25:29-30

# More than a family squabble

### REBEKAH'S PLAN

Jacob was his mom's (Rebekah's) favorite.

Esau was the apple of his dad's (Isaac's) eye.

Rebekah overheard the elderly, and nearly blind, Isaac having a quiet word with Esau.

"Esau, my son," Isaac said slowly, "prepare my favorite meal, game pie. I'll eat it and then give you my special blessing."

Rebekah went straight to Jacob with this news.

"Now, Jacob," schemed Rebekah, "do as I say, and the blessing will be yours."

So Jacob picked two fat young goats from the flock. Rebekah made them into a tasty dish — just the sort that she knew Isaac loved.

### "I'M SMOOTH-SKINNED"

"Now, Jacob," whispered Rebekah, "this is your chance. Give this to your dad to eat."

"But," protested Jacob, "I'm smooth-skinned, while Esau is hairy. Dad may be half blind, but he'll know I'm not Esau when he touches me."

Quick as a flash, Rebekah said, "Don't worry. Put on these clothes — they're Esau's best, and wrap these goat skins around your hands and neck. They'll fool your dad."

The trick worked. Isaac thought Jacob was Esau and gave him his special blessing.

"Cursed be everyone who
curses you, and blessed be
everyone who blesses you!"

Genesis 27:29

43

# Jacob leaves home

44

### Escaping from Esau

When Esau found out about the trick Rebekah and Jacob played on Isaac, he was mad with anger. He was out to kill Jacob.

*And he dreamed that there was a ladder set up on the earth . . . and the angels of God were ascending and descending on it.*

Genesis 28:12

Rebekah told Jacob, "Esau knows you cheated him out of his birthright and blessing. Now he's after your blood. Leave here and go to my brother, Laban, so Esau has time to cool down."

On his way to his Uncle Laban, Jacob spent the night at Bethel. He slept under the stars and used a stone as his pillow.

JACOB'S DREAM

That night Jacob had a dream he never forgot.

He saw angels going up and down a huge ladder. God stood above the ladder.

Then God spoke to Jacob:

"I am the God of Abraham, your grandfather; the God of Isaac, your father.

"I will give the land you are now asleep on to your descendants.

"They will be as many as the dust of the earth.

"I will be with you. I will protect you."

# The cheat is cheated

*So Jacob served seven years for Rachel, and they seemed to him but a few days because of the love he had for her.*

Genesis 29:20

## LEAH AND RACHEL

Jacob arrived at Laban's farm where he became a shepherd.

Laban had two daughters. The elder daughter, Leah, had lovely eyes, and the younger daughter, Rachel, was graceful and beautiful. Jacob fell in love with Rachel.

## A SEVEN-YEAR-LONG ENGAGEMENT

Laban promised Jacob that he could marry his daughter Rachel. But first, Jacob had to work for him for seven years. Jacob loved Rachel so much that the seven years passed in a moment.

*Leah's eyes were lovely,
and Rachel was graceful
and beautiful.*

Genesis 29:17

## LABAN'S TRICK

After seven years, Jacob said to Laban, "Now I can marry
Rachel."

So Laban laid on a great party. Then, in the evening,
Laban gave Jacob one of his daughters who was wearing a veil.

In the morning Jacob went to Laban, white-hot with
anger:

"You gave me your daughter Leah. But I wanted Rachel!"

"Ah," replied Jacob, "we have a custom that the younger
daughter can't marry before the older daughter is married.

"Work for me for seven more years and Rachel is yours."

Jacob had no option but to agree.

# Rachel's theft

48

*Rachel stole her father's household gods.*

Genesis 31:19

## HUNT THE IDOL

After Jacob's flocks of goats and sheep had become very numerous, God spoke to Jacob again:

"Jacob. Go back to the land where you were raised. I will be with you."

As they left, Rachel stole Laban's precious idols. Even though Laban came after Jacob, looking for his idols, he never found them. Rachel had hidden them in her camel's saddle.

## FRIENDS AGAIN

Jacob was terrified to see Esau again, but Esau ran to meet him, crying with joy.

# Joseph's startling dreams

### Introduction

This chapter is all about the life of Joseph.

It starts with a teenager having two startling dreams.

Joseph's life takes an unpromising turn when he is thrown into a dry well by his brothers. Then he becomes a slave in Egypt.

Joseph's see-saw life takes a turn for the better when he is put in charge of the home of Potiphar, a very important Egyptian soldier.

Next, a bizarre twist of events lands Joseph in prison for three years.

Who could have guessed that he would then become vice president of Egypt, save the Egyptians from a seven-year famine, and arrange for his father and brothers to live with him in Egypt?

# Joseph the dreamer

50

## DAD'S FAVORITE SON

Joseph, Jacob's favorite son, worked with his brothers as a shepherd. Once, when he was 17, he gave his father a bad report about his brothers. The brothers were furious. Then, to show how much he loved Joseph, Jacob gave him a special robe with long sleeves. The brothers were green with envy.

**Joseph's coat**

*What did it look like?*
The coat which Jacob made for Joseph is popularly known as Joseph's "coat of many colors." This comes from the translation of this verse in the King James Version of the Bible.

Instead of colors, the robe may have had stripes, oraments, or long sleeves.

*What did it mean?*
The robe was a mark of Jacob's favoritism for the son he loved best.

This coat may have shown that Jacob planned to leave his wealth to Joseph after he died.

## SHEAVES

One morning, Joseph told his brothers about a dream he'd just had.

"We were in the field tying up bundles of wheat. Then my bundle stood up and your 11 bundles of wheat gathered around mine. Then your bundles bowed to my bundle."

"So you think you're going to be a king and rule over us," mocked his brothers.

*He [Joseph] said to them, "Listen to this dream that I dreamed. There we were, binding sheaves in the field . . . Your sheaves . . . bowed down to my sheaf."*

Genesis 37:6-7

# Dreams don't seem to come true

52

> *"Look, I have had another dream: the sun, the moon, and eleven stars were bowing down to me."*
>
> Genesis 37:9

### THE STARS

Joseph had another dream. This was the last straw.

This time, Joseph told his brothers, "The sun, the moon, and 11 stars were all bowing down to me."

When Joseph told his father, Jacob told him off, saying, "Do you expect your mother and me, along with your brothers, to bow down to you?"

Worst of all, the brothers hated Joseph even more because Jacob took such notice of Joseph's dream.

## INTO A WELL

Jacob told Joseph to check on his 11 brothers, who had gone to Shechem with flocks of sheep.

Joseph found them at Dothan. But they saw him coming and hatched a plot.

"Let's kill him. We'll tell dad that a bear killed him," they schemed.

"No," said the oldest brother, Reuben, "don't hurt him. Just throw him into this empty well."

So into the well went Joseph.

When Reuben left, the other brothers sold Joseph to some Ishmaelite traders.

*Genesis chapter 37 verses 25 to 36 and chapter 39 verses 1 to 20*

# Sold into slavery

**Jacob mourns for Joseph**

*Tearing clothes*
When Jacob thought that Joseph had been killed by a wild animal he tore his clothes. When Reuben found that Joseph had been taken out of the well he tore his clothes. This was a sign of deep sorrow.

*Wearing sackcloth*
Another way to express sadness over someone's death in those days was to wear coarse and uncomfortable sackcloth instead of normal clothes.

**Come, let us sell him to the Ishmaelites, and not lay our hands on him, for he is our brother.**

*Genesis 37:27*

## JACOB'S SADNESS

When the 11 brothers returned to Jacob they showed him Joseph's special robe. They had stripped him of it and dipped it in goat's blood.

"Yes, dad. Isn't it sad. Some wild animal obviously killed Joseph," the brothers lied.

Jacob tore his clothes and dressed in sackcloth. He was so sad that nothing and nobody could comfort him. "I'll be overcome with sadness until my dying day," said Jacob.

## POTIPHAR

The Ishmaelite traders took Joseph to Egypt and sold him to an important soldier called Potiphar, who was captain of the palace guard.

All would have been fine for Joseph but for Potiphar's wife. Because Joseph refused her advances, Potiphar's wife lied about him and convinced Potiphar to throw Joseph into prison.

# Joseph in prison

56

*"I also had a dream: there were three cake baskets on my head."*

Genesis 40:16

### THE WINE WAITER'S DREAM

In prison Joseph knew that God was with him and still looking after him.

Even the prison warden liked Joseph, and he was put in charge of the other prisoners.

The king's wine waiter was also in prison and told Joseph about a dream he had.

"I saw a vine which had three branches. I squeezed juice from its grapes into the king's cup," recounted the wine waiter.

"This means," explained Joseph, "that in three days you will be freed."

"And when you're free, remember me. Tell the king about me so I will be freed as well," added Joseph.

### THE BAKER'S DREAM

Then the king's baker, who was also in prison, told Joseph his dream.

"On my head, I saw three baskets and birds ate food from the top basket," said the baker, hopefully.

*Genesis chapter 39 verse 21 to chapter 41 verse 4*

"In three days time," Joseph told him, "the king will kill you and birds will eat you."

Both these dreams came true, exactly as Joseph had said. But no one helped Joseph to be released from prison.

## THE KING'S DREAM

Two years later, unknown to Joseph, the king also had a dream. It was all about seven skinny cows gobbling up seven fat cows!

*And there came up out of the Nile seven sleek and fat cows . . . Then seven other cows, ugly and thin, came up out of the Nile after them.*

Genesis 41:2-3

# A prisoner advises a king

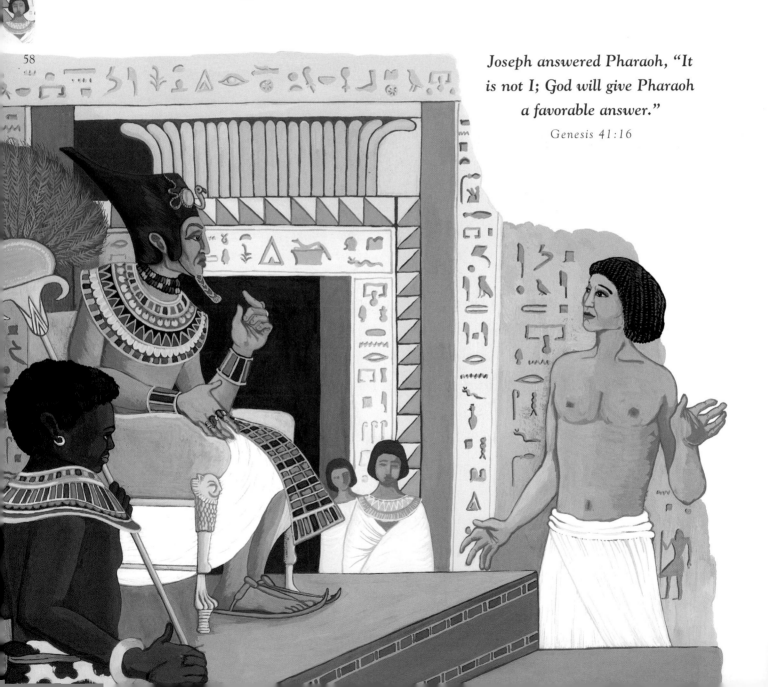

Joseph answered Pharaoh, "It is not I; God will give Pharaoh a favorable answer."

Genesis 41:16

*Genesis chapter 41 verse 5 to chapter 41 verse 34*

## THE KING'S SECOND DREAM

The following night the king had another dream.

He saw seven good heads of grain on one stalk. Then he saw seven thin and shriveled heads of grain. The thin grain gobbled up the good grain.

"Come on now," bellowed the king to his magicians and wise advisors, "I've told you my dreams. You tell me what they mean!"

The silence was deafening. Nobody could interpret the king's dreams.

## THE WINE WAITER REMEMBERS

"Your majesty," said the wine waiter hesitantly, "when I was in prison the baker and I had dreams. A young Hebrew man told us what they meant."

"Send for that man," ordered the king.

## BOTH DREAMS MEAN THE SAME THING

"The king's calling for you, Joseph," beamed the friendly prison guard. "You'd better have a quick wash, shave and change of clothes."

Joseph explained the dreams: Egypt was going to have seven years of great harvests followed by seven years when nothing would grow.

# Joseph's brothers come to Egypt

60

### JOSEPH BECOMES VICE PRESIDENT

The king made Joseph the second most powerful person in the land. He put Joseph in charge of organizing everything so that there would be enough food to last during the seven bad harvests.

"Here you are, Joseph. Here's my special ring with my own personal royal seal on it.

"Here's a set of best linen clothes for you to wear.

"And here's a gold chain for you.

"And here's the second best chariot in the land for you to ride in."

### A DREAM COMES TRUE

Ten men came before Joseph. They didn't recognize Joseph, but Joseph knew that they were 10 of his 11 brothers. They bowed before him, just like the sheaves and stars had done in his dreams.

"We've come all the way from Canaan to buy food, sir," the men pleaded.

Joseph pretended not to know them. Then he ordered them to return to their homeland and bring back the one missing brother, whose name was Benjamin. Joseph put Simeon in prison as a hostage.

*When Joseph came
home, they brought him
the present . . . and
bowed to the ground
before him.*

Genesis 43:26

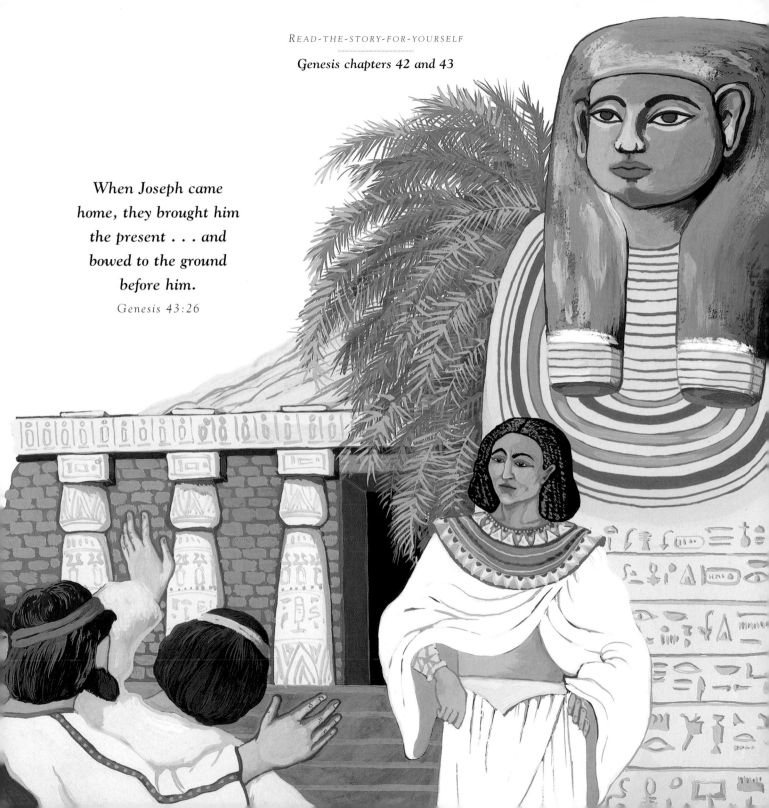

# Joseph and his brothers

62

### ELEVEN BROTHERS GO TO EGYPT

The nine brothers returned with sacks of grain to Canaan, and, with great difficulty, persuaded their father Jacob to allow Benjamin to return with them to Joseph.

### JOSEPH'S TRAP

Joseph pretended to allow the eleven brothers to return home a second time, laden with as much grain as they could carry.

He had secretly told one of his servants to put his silver cup in Benjamin's sack.

After they had left for Canaan Joseph sent a servant after them.

*He searched, beginning with the eldest and ending with the youngest, and the cup was found in Benjamin's sack.*

Genesis 44:12

**Genesis chapters 44 and 45**

63

"Whoever has stolen my master's silver cup will be his slave," the servant threatened.

The cup was, of course, found in Benjamin's sack.

"Please, sir," pleaded the brothers, "let Benjamin return home. Or else it will break his father's heart."

JOSEPH SAYS WHO HE IS

With only his brothers in the room, Joseph then broke down and wept.

He told his eleven brothers, "I am your brother, Joseph."

The eleven brothers were stunned.

Then they hugged each other with joy and amazement.

*Then he fell upon his brother Benjamin's neck and wept, while Benjamin wept.*

Genesis 45:14

*Genesis chapter 45 verse 9 to chapter 49 verse 28*

# Jacob goes to Egypt

64

Joseph told his eleven brothers to go back to Jacob,
who was also called Israel. "Tell him all that had
happened to me — how I'm now vice president
of Egypt. I'll look after you all during the next
five years of the famine," promised Joseph.

Jacob was pleased to hear this
unbelievably good news. He said, "I'm
going to go to Egypt to see Joseph
before I die."

## WELCOME JACOB

When the king of Egypt heard
about Joseph's brothers, he gave them
the best of everything in Egypt.

When Jacob arrived, Joseph and Jacob hugged each
other. Joseph brought his two sons to meet the
grandfather they had never seen.

Jacob put his hands gently on the heads of Joseph's
sons, and blessed them.

*Joseph said to his father,
"They are my sons . . .
and he said, "Bring
them to me, please, that
I may bless them."*

Genesis 48:9

# HEBREW SCRIPTURES

## Chapter 4: From the Bible book of Exodus

# Moses and the great escape

INTRODUCTION

*This chapter tells the gripping story of the Israelites escaping from Egypt.*

*It is told through the eyes of Moses. Many remarkable things happened to him in his life. To start with, his survival as a baby was against all the odds. That's because the king of Egypt had commanded that all baby boys born to the Israelites should be thrown into the River Nile.*

*Then Moses had the never-to-be-forgotten experience in the desert of seeing a burning bush that somehow did not burn up.*

*Moses was given the thankless task of tackling the king of Egypt. Each time the king refused to let the Israelites go, God sent a plague to devastate the Egyptians.*

*The dramatic climax of the escape from Egypt comes in the parting of the waters of the Red Sea.*

# The Israelites grow

*The daughter of Pharaoh
came down to bathe at
the river . . . she saw
the child. He was crying,
and she took pity on him.*

Exodus 2:5,6

## FROM 70 PEOPLE TO A GREAT NATION

When Jacob arrived in Egypt, his eleven sons and their families were 70 people. The people of Israel had many children and their number grew.

## A NEW KING OF EGYPT

When a new king began to rule Egypt, he said, "These Israelites are going to overrun us. Kill all their baby boys! Throw them into the River Nile."

## MOSES IS BORN

The brave Hebrew midwives refused to do what the king commanded. One Israelite mom hid her baby boy in a basket among the tall grass of the River Nile. Miriam, Moses' sister, watched over him. The king's daughter discovered him, felt sorry for him, and adopted him as her own son.

**Moses**

*What does "Moses" mean?*
"Moses" an Egyptian name means "is born."

The king's daughter explained that she called the baby "Moses" because she "drew him out of the water" (Exodus 2:10). This is a word play as "Moses" sounds like the Hebrew word for "drew out."

Just as Moses was rescued from the Nile, so God delivered the people from the Red Sea.

# Moses runs away from Egypt

68

## MOSES SUPPORTS HIS PEOPLE

Moses grew up in the king's palace, but he loved his own people, the Israelites. He couldn't stand the way the Egyptians forced them to work as slaves and treated them so cruelly. One day Moses saw an Israelite being beaten, so he killed the Egyptian and hid his body in the sand. But news about this soon spread. Moses ran for his life.

## THE BURNING BUSH

One day Moses saw flames of fire coming out of a bush. But the bush wasn't burned up. Moses said, "I must take a closer look at this! How can a bush have flames and not be burned?"

## RESCUE MISSION

Then God spoke to Moses from the bush,

"Moses, Moses! Take off your sandals.

"You are standing on holy ground.

"I am the God of Abraham, the God of Isaac and the God of Jacob.

"My people, the Israelites, are slaves. I now order you to go to the king of Egypt and tell him to let my people go."

Then Moses said, "I must turn aside and look at this great sight, and see why the bush is not burned up."

Exodus 3:3

69

# "Let my people go"

*But Pharaoh said,
"Who is the Lord, that
I should heed him . . .
and let Israel go?"*

Exodus 5:2

Moses could not believe his ears. "I'm no great man, oh God. How can I possibly go to the king of Egypt and lead the people out of Egypt?" Moses protested.

God replied, "I will be with you to help you do this. You will lead the people out of Egypt. Then you will all worship me on this mountain."

## AARON SPEAKS FOR MOSES

"Please, God," Moses said, "can't you send someone else to do this. I'm not even good at speaking."

"Your brother, Aaron, can speak for you. You tell him what I tell you, and Aaron will speak to the king," God replied.

## "LET MY PEOPLE GO"

Moses and Aaron went to the king of Egypt. They said to him, "This is what the God of Israel says, 'Let my people go, so they can hold a festival for me in the desert.'"

## THE KING IS NOT AMUSED

"How dare you stop the slaves from working," raged the king.

"Don't give the people any more straw to make the bricks with," the king ordered the slave masters. "But make sure they still make as many bricks."

"That'll teach them," the king thought to himself.

*But the king of Egypt said to them, "Moses and Aaron, why are you taking the people away from their work?"*

Exodus 5:4

# Miserable Moses

The Israelites were fed up with Moses for landing them with such extra work.

Moses was fed up with God. "Look what trouble you've brought on us, God," Moses complained.

"Don't worry," replied God. "I will use my great power and the king of Egypt will let my people go."

**Exodus chapter 5 verse 22 to chapter 8 verse 15**

*And the frogs came
up and covered the
land of Egypt.*

Exodus 8:6

*. . . and the fish in the
river died. The river
stank so that the
Egyptians could not
drink its water, and
there was blood
throughout the whole
land of Egypt.*

Exodus 7:21

PLAGUE NUMBER ONE: WATER TURNS TO BLOOD
"I will punish the Egyptians in terrible ways," God
promised.

"Tell Aaron," said God, "to stretch out his staff
over the rivers, ponds, canals, and pools of Egypt."
Every drop of water was turned into blood.

PLAGUE NUMBER TWO: FROGS
"Tell the king that the land will be filled with frogs if
he does not let my people go," said God.

The frogs went everywhere: in the king's palace,
under the beds, in the ovens, behind the saucepans, on
the sandals — one even sat on the king's throne!

# Plagues galore!

74

## PLAGUES THREE TO NINE

There were ten plagues in all. The next were:

Plague number three: gnats

Plague number four: flies

Plague number five: disease on farm animals

Plague number six: boils

Plague number seven: hail

Plague number eight: locusts

Plague number nine: darkness

*It caused festering boils
on humans and animals.*

Exodus 9:10

## ONLY EGYPTIANS SUFFER

Each plague hit only the Egyptians. The worst
hailstorm in history destroyed everything in the
Egyptian fields. But in the land of Goshen, where the
Israelites lived, there were no hailstones.

## THE KING'S STUBBORN HEART

As each plague ravaged the Egyptians, the king
acted in the same way.

When the plague of locusts
had gobbled up every leaf from
every plant on Egyptian
land, the king sent for
Moses and Aaron and said,
"Get rid of these locusts. I
promise I'll let you go. Only
get rid of the locusts."

As soon as the locusts
disappeared the king changed
his mind.

*All the dust of the earth
turned into gnats
throughout the whole
land of Egypt.*

Exodus 8:17

# The last plague

76

## THE TENTH PLAGUE

The tenth and final plague was the plague to end all plagues.

Moses told the king, "This is what God says: 'About midnight tonight I will go through all Egypt. Every firstborn son in the land of Egypt will die. The firstborn son of the king, who sits on his throne, will die. Even the firstborn of the slave girl grinding grain will die. Also the firstborn farm animals will die. There will be loud crying everywhere in Egypt. It will be worse than any time before or after this.'"

*"Every firstborn in the land of Egypt shall die."*

*Exodus 11:5*

*Exodus chapters 11 and 12*

# A midnight to remember

### A STUBBORN KING

Of course, Moses and Aaron knew what would
happen. Aaron would warn the king about what God
was about to do, but the king would be unmoved. The
king had a stubborn hard heart. He would not let
God's people leave his country.

That night, at midnight it happened. Pharaoh
woke up. There was the sound of loud
crying across the whole land.

*And he [Pharaoh] did
not let the people of
Israel go out of his land.*
Exodus 11:10

# The great escape

The king called Moses and Aaron in the middle of the night. "Get out of here," he commanded. "Take all the Israelites with you, and all your animals. Begone!" There were no signposts to help Moses lead the hundreds of thousands of God's people out of Egypt. God led them through the desert toward the Red Sea.

### A PILLAR OF CLOUD AND A PILLAR OF FIRE

God guided Moses and showed him which way to take.  During the day God went ahead of the Israelites in a pillar of cloud. During the night God was in a pillar of fire which threw light on the track to follow.

### "RAISE YOUR STAFF"

Just as he had done before, the king changed his mind. Moses and God's people now had the Egyptian army advancing behind them and the Red Sea in front of them. Was this the end? Would it be a watery grave or would the soldiers in the king's 600 best chariots make mincemeat of them?

Then it happened. As Moses raised his staff and held it over the sea, the sea split. There was a wall of water on both sides of them. But the Israelites went across on dry land.

*God went in front of them in a pillar of cloud by day . . . and in a pillar of fire by night.*

Exodus 13:21

# Songs of praise

80

### "WE'VE ESCAPED"

The Egyptian soldiers tried to follow the Israelites, but their chariot wheels stuck in the mud and the Egyptians could not escape when the walls of water closed in on them. It was a miracle the Israelites would never forget. They had escaped from Egypt. God had led them.

### THE SONG OF MIRIAM AND MOSES

Moses and the Israelites sang to celebrate their escape:

"I will sing to God, who gives me strength. God has saved us; he has led us out of slavery in Egypt."

### REACH FOR THE TAMBOURINES

This was a day for the tambourines. Miriam, Aaron's sister, banging her tambourine for all she was worth, led the women in their song of praise to God: "Sing to God, sing praises to God. God has thrown the army into the sea. We're free, we're free."

*Then the prophet Miriam, Aaron's sister, took a tambourine in her hand.*

Exodus 15:20

## HEBREW SCRIPTURES

*Chapter 5: From the Bible books of Exodus, Numbers, Deuteronomy, and Joshua*

# God's people journey through the desert

### INTRODUCTION

*Life in the desert was certainly very different from being a slave in Egypt.*

*But Moses was faced with so many new problems. Where was there water to be found in the desert? What about food for 600,000 people every day? Then there was the constant grumbling and complaining of the Israelites. Worst of all Moses even found them worshiping a golden calf.*

*Moses, who did not live to see the end of the journey, appointed Joshua to lead the people after he was dead.*

*Joshua sent spies into the land of Canaan, then led battles to capture its cities, including the important city of Jericho.*

82

# Problems in the desert

Things did not go smoothly for Moses after he led God's people out of their slavery in Egypt.

### NO FOOD

When their food ran out, the Israelites immediately blamed Moses. "Did you bring us out into this parched desert to die of hunger," they said to Moses accusingly.

Moses told them that they were grumbling against God when they grumbled against him and Aaron.

"God will provide you with meat in the evenings.

"God will provide you with bread in the mornings," Moses assured the people.

Amazingly this happened. In the evening, tasty birds called quails flew in on the wind. They were easy to catch. In the mornings the people collected thin flakes like frost from the ground. "What's this?" they asked Moses.

"It's bread that God has given you to eat," replied Moses.

## Quails

*How did they arrive?*
Quails are a small game bird and are considered to be a great delicacy.

Quails migrate in very large flocks. They are carried along by the prevailing winds.

*How were quails caught?*
Quails are not very good at flying. Often they travel only three or four feet above the ground.

No water

Then the Israelites ran out of water. Once again they put the blame on Moses.

God told Moses to hit a rock at Mount Sinai with the same staff that he raised to part the Red Sea. Then streams of water gushed out from the rock.

*"Strike the rock, and water will come out of it, so that the people may drink."*

Exodus 17:6

# A golden calf

84     God's people did many wrong things as they traveled through the desert from Egypt to the land of Canaan.

    One of the worst things they did happened while they were waiting for Moses to come down from Mount Sinai where he was receiving the Ten Commandments.

*He [Aaron] took the gold from them, formed it in a mold, and cast an image of a calf.*

Exodus 32:4

## "GIVE ME YOUR GOLD"

"Go on, Aaron," urged the people, "make us gods to lead us. As for Moses, who knows what's happened to him?"

"Right," replied Aaron, "give me all the gold you can find. Get all the gold earrings you can lay your hands on — from your wives, your sons and your daughters."

Before he had time to think about his wrong actions, Aaron had melted down all the gold and made a beautiful, golden idol, in the shape of a calf.

"Here you are, people of Israel," said Aaron, as the people bowed down in front of the golden calf. "This is the god who brought you out of Egypt!" lied Aaron.

## ENTER MOSES

When Moses came down from the top of the mountain, he saw the golden calf. The people were dancing around it.

Then every eye turned towards Moses. He was furious.

He broke the two tablets of stone he was carrying with the Ten Commandments written on both sides.

He snatched hold of the golden calf and melted it down in the fire. He ground all the gold into powder, threw the powder into water, and made the people drink that water.

# Spy out the land

86

### "HAVE A LOOK AT CANAAN"

God told Moses, "Send one leader from each tribe into the land of Canaan to explore it."

"See if the land is good for fruit or grazing sheep," Moses instructed them.

"Take note of the people who live there," added Moses.

### THE NEGATIVE REPORT

After forty days the spies came back with a huge cluster of grapes as well as pomegranates and figs.

*"Send men to spy out the land of Canaan."*

Numbers 13:2

***They also brought some***
***pomegranates and figs.***

*Numbers 13:23*

All the spies agreed that the land was lush and perfect for growing fruit.

But nearly all the spies said, "Don't even think about attacking this land!

"The people are very tall and we felt like grasshoppers beside them.

"The towns are so well fortified with their high walls that we wouldn't stand a chance if we tried to capture them."

## THE POSITIVE REPORT

Only Joshua and Caleb gave a positive report about the land. They said, "We can take the land for ourselves. We should advance and capture it. We can do it!"

# End of an era

88

### HELLO JOSHUA

Moses was old and knew that his days were numbered. In front of all of the people he said, "God has told me that I will not be going with you into the Promised Land. But don't be afraid. God will go with you."

Then Moses told Joshua to take over from him as leader of God's people.

*Then Moses summoned Joshua . . . in the sight of all Israel.*

*Deuteronomy 31:7*

89

## GOODBYE MOSES

Moses climbed to the top of Mount Nebo and looked at all the land God had promised Abraham that God would give to the people. Then Moses, who had been such a close friend of God, died. Moses was buried in the land of Moab, but nobody knows his burial place. The Israelites wept for Moses for thirty days.

*Then Moses went up from the plains of Moab to Mount Nebo.*

Deuteronomy 34:1

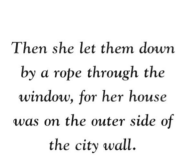

*Then she let them down by a rope through the window, for her house was on the outer side of the city wall.*

Joshua 2:15

# Spies sent to Jericho

## JOSHUA TAKES OVER

Moses had died. Joshua had been appointed to take his place.

God said to Joshua, "Be strong and brave. Lead these people to inherit the land that I promised to their ancestors. And remember, I will be with you always, wherever you go."

## HELPFUL RAHAB

Joshua wanted to capture the city of Jericho. He wisely sent out two spies to see its precise strength.

The two spies stayed with a woman from Jericho, named Rahab. But someone told the king of Jericho, "Some of those Israelites have entered our city."

"Quick," said Rahab, "the soldiers are looking for you. Go up to the roof. Lie down on the floor." Then Rahab hid them under stalks of flax.

When the soldiers hammered on Rahab's door she said, "Yes, I did see some men, but they left before the city gate closed."

## SECRET SIGNAL

Rahab let the spies down the city wall with a red rope from her window. The spies told Rahab, "Tie this red rope to your window and everyone with you will be kept safe when we attack Jericho."

# The battle for Jericho

### A STRANGE ENCOUNTER

As Joshua came close to Jericho he was confronted by a man who had a menacing sword in his hand.

"Friend or foe?" stammered Joshua.

"I," the man replied with great dignity, "am the commander of God's army."

No, this wasn't a ghost! Joshua knew he was face-to-face with a messenger from God.

Joshua seemed hardly surprised when he was told, "Take off your sandals. You are standing on holy ground."

*Once when Joshua was by Jericho, he looked up and saw a man standing before him with a drawn sword in his hand.*

Joshua 5:13

### STRANGE TACTICS

Joshua was given a set of very odd-sounding orders by God:

"March round the city of Jericho with your army, once a day, for six days.

"March in front of the Holy Ark.

"March with seven priests carrying trumpets made from rams' horns."

BLOW THE TRUMPET

"On the seventh day tell the priests to give one long blast on their trumpets," continued God. "Make sure everyone gives a huge cheer! Then the wall will fall down. And the people will go straight into the city."

And that's exactly what happened.

RAHAB IS NOT FORGOTTEN

Rahab remembered to tie the red rope to her window, and her family was kept safe.

THE CITY OF AI

Joshua went on to capture the city of Ai by using a cunning ambush, but that's another story.

*The troops in ambush rose quickly out of their place and rushed forward.*

Joshua 8:19

**The city of Jericho**

Jericho is naturally protected by mountains. The Jordan river and underground tributaries create a green oasis in the desert. Located in the middle of Palestine, Jericho was an important city for invaders to control.

Did Joshua really destroy the city? Some archaeologists claim the city was already in ruins centuries before Joshua arrived. Others say there was a fire at about the time Joshua lived.

Since the city walls had been destroyed by earthquakes 17 times before Joshua and his people saw Jericho, it's possible that another quake occurred close to the time of their arrival and was seen as God's doing.

# Joshua is tricked

94

### DIPLOMACY NOT WAR

Not everyone in Canaan resisted Joshua and the Israelites. One group of people, the Gibeonites, decided on diplomacy rather than war.

### THE CLEVER PLAN

They knew they could never defeat Joshua, so they decided to trick him into having pity on them.

They searched high and low for anything that was old, musty, torn, worn, cracked, or mended. "I've found those moth-eaten sandals I should have thrown out years ago," cried one of the people of Gibeon.

They put frayed sacks on their donkeys, they wore smelly old clothes, and they put falling apart sandals on their feet.

### "LOOK AT OUR BREAD"

"Here's some really stale, moldy bread," a delighted Gibeonite exclaimed.

When they met Joshua they said, "Look how poor we are. See how moldy our bread is. We've come such a long way. Will you, please, make a peace pact with us?"

"That won't do," the Israelites replied, "we can't make peace with you if you live near us."

The Gibeonites had an answer for everything. "Oh," a quick-thinking Gibeonite replied, "don't worry yourself about that. We'll be your servants."

The Israelites checked out their story by trying some of their bread. They spat it out of their mouths in disgust as soon as they tasted just how moldy it was.

## A PROMISE OF PEACE

So Joshua promised not to attack the Gibeonites.

Only later did he learn that they lived very close to where he was. He had been completely taken in. He also remembered what he had forgotten. He'd not asked God what to do.

The Gibeonites carried water and cut wood for the Israelites, and were left unharmed.

*The inhabitants of Gibeon . . . took . . . worn-out clothes; and all their provisions were dry and moldy.*

Joshua 9:3,5

95

*Joshua chapter 21 verses 1 to 4, chapter 23, and chapter 24*

# Goodbye Joshua

96

### SETTLING DOWN

Under Joshua's dynamic leadership, the people of Israel settled down in the land of Canaan.

The different tribes were given different parts of the land to live in.

The Levites had to sort out where they were going to live. They went and asked Eleazar the priest. They were given towns to live in and pastures to support them, just as God had promised.

### FAREWELL SPEECH

God had given the people a safe country to live in under Joshua's wise leadership.

Now Joshua was very old. He knew that he would soon die.

Joshua collected everyone together and told them: "You must throw away the false gods that you worshiped. Love God with all your heart. Keep on obeying God's laws and you will prosper."

"Yes," agreed the people, "we will serve our God."

*He [Joshua] took a large stone, and set it up under the oak in the sanctuary of God.*

Joshua 24:26

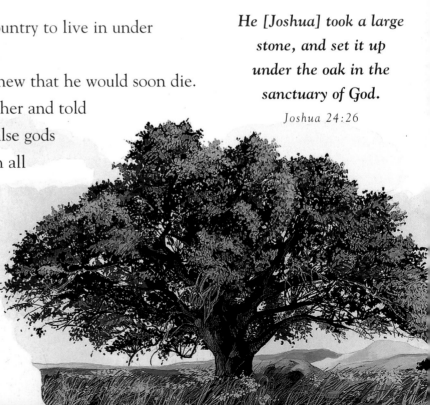

# HEBREW SCRIPTURES

*Chapter 6: From the Bible books of Exodus, Leviticus, Numbers,*
*and Deuteronomy*

# Learning God's way

## INTRODUCTION

*The Bible books of Exodus, Leviticus, Numbers and Deuteronomy tell how*
*Moses led God's people through the desert. As they traveled, God gave them*
*laws. Some laws explained how to worship and how to build a holy meeting*
*tent to carry through the desert. Special objects in the tent reminded people*
*about God.*

*Some laws helped the people get organized into groups, called the twelve*
*tribes of Israel. The Ten Commandments were an important set of laws to help*
*people relate to God and to each other.*

*Many laws taught the people kindness, respect, justice and generosity. For*
*example, they were to look after people who didn't have anyone to help them.*
*There were laws about taking care of the land and laws about what foods to eat.*

*The laws were a gift from God. They helped the people to live well, close*
*to one another and close to God.*

### The twelve tribes

The twelve tribes of Israel made up God's people, the Israelites. Each tribe was named after one of the twelve sons of Jacob.

They lived in their tribes or families in the desert.

They pitched their tents in a square formation with God's Tent of Meeting in their center.

Three tribes were on the east side, three on the south side, three on the west side and three on the north side.

*Exodus chapter 26, and chapter 27 verses 9 to 19*

# The holy meeting tent

99

*"You shall make the
tabernacle with ten curtains
of fine twisted linen, and
blue, purple, and crimson
yarns; you shall make them
with cherubim skillfully
worked into them."*

Exodus 26:1

# Inside God's tent

### The Holy Meeting Tent

God gave Moses many very detailed instructions about constructing a special tent. Moses said, "I call it the meeting tent. It is where God meets with his people." Only the priests could enter the tent.

Inside this meeting tent were three carefully made things.

*"They shall make an ark of acacia wood."*

Exodus 25:10

### The ark

This was also known as the covenant box. A man called Bezalel made it of acacia wood. He overlaid the wooden box with gold.

On its lid Bezalel hammered gold into the shape of two creatures with wings. They faced each other and their wings spread across the top of the box.

The two flat stones with the Ten Commandments on them were placed inside the ark.

*"You shall make a table
of acacia wood."*

Exodus 25:23

101

## THE TABLE

A table, made out of acacia wood and covered with pure gold, also stood inside God's holy meeting tent. On this table golden plates had bread on them that was offered to God.

## THE LAMPSTAND

God also told Moses, "Make a lampstand out of pure gold." It had to have three branches on each side, making seven in all. These became seven small oil lamps.

*"You shall make a
lampstand of pure gold."*

# Sacrifices for God

102

### THE COURTYARD

Outside God's tent, but enclosed in a fence of curtains was a large courtyard. In this courtyard God told Moses to have two things made.

### THE ALTAR

God told Moses to have a square-shaped bronze altar made. Each corner of the altar had to stick out like a horn. It was made out of acacia wood, covered in bronze. This was used for burning the sacrifices — the sheep and goats.

Special pots were made to remove the ashes. Shovels and bowls were made for sprinkling the blood. Then there were large meat forks, as well as pans for carrying the burning wood. Everything had to be made of bronze.

*"You shall make horns for it [the altar] on its four corners."*

Exodus 27:2

xodus chapter 25 verses 1 to 40, and, chapter 30 verses 17-21

*"You shall make pots for it to receive its ashes, and shovels and basins and forks and firepans; you shall make all its utensils of bronze."*

Exodus 27:3

### Poles and rings

All the objects inside and outside God's meeting tent were portable. They could be easily carried around by the Israelites as they pitched camp in different places in the desert.

The ark of the covenant, the table and the bronze altar were all fitted with four rings through which two carrying poles fitted. In this way everything could be easily carried.

### THE BRONZE BOWL

Before the priests entered the Tent of Meeting or sacrificed any of the animals God ordered that they should wash their hands and feet. Water for this was put in a large bronze bowl which had its own bronze stand.

# Special clothes

104

### PRIESTS

The people who looked after the sacrifices around God's special tent were called priests. They had special, holy work to do for God, so God ordered that they should wear special clothes.

God told Moses, "Tell your brother Aaron and his children to serve me as priests. Make holy clothes for Aaron which will give him beauty and honor."

Aaron was the first chief priest and was called the high priest.

*"You shall make the robe of the ephod [linen garment] all of blue."*

Exodus 28:31

*"You shall make the checkered tunic of fine linen, and you shall make a turban of fine linen, and you shall make a sash embroidered with needlework."*

Exodus 28:39

*Exodus chapter 28 verses 1 to 43*

### The Day of Atonement

*The first goat*

Once a year, on the Day of Atonement, the high priest sprinkled blood from a killed goat on the ark of the covenant in God's meeting tent.

This was God's way of teaching the people how innocent blood was shed instead of the people who had sinned against God.

*The second goat*

The high priest then took another goat, placed hands on its head, and confessed the sins of God's people. This goat was known as the scapegoat. This goat was set free and, symbolically, carried away the peoples' sins.

*"He made the breastplate, in skilled work . . . of blue, purple, and crimson yarns, and of fine, twisted linen."*

*Exodus 39:8*

## CHEST COVERING

God also told Moses that Aaron had to wear a special chest covering.

It had four rows of beautiful gems on it.

The first row of jewels had a ruby, a topaz and a yellow quartz.

The second row had a turquoise, a sapphire and an emerald.

The third row had a jacinth, an agate and an amethyst.

On each of the twelve jewels was engraved the name of one of the twelve tribes of Israel.

*"There were twelve stones with names corresponding to the names of the sons of Israel; they were like signets, each engraved with its name, for the twelve tribes."*

*Exodus 39:14*

# Everybody is involved

106

Each of the twelve tribes of Israel brought gifts for God's meeting tent. Each tribe brought the same number and same kind of gifts.

## THE GIFTS

Each tribe brought one silver plate, one silver sprinkling bowl, one gold dish, one young bull, one ram and one lamb for a burnt offering, one goat for a sin offering, two oxen, five rams, five goats, and five lambs as a fellowship offering.

### Sacrifices

*The burnt offering*
The animal was killed and completely burned.
This symbolized the wish to be rid of sin.

*The sin offering*
A goat was sacrificed. This symbolized the sins of the Israelites being "paid off" by the goat.

*The fellowship offering*
An animal was sacrificed. This symbolized the people's wish to give thanks.

107

### Festivals

Trumpets were to be blown to announce festivals and celebrations.

These festivals, which were times of great celebration, reminded God's people of God's great care for them.

*The Feast of Trumpets*
This celebrated the New Year.

*New Moon Festival*
This was held at the start of each month.

*The Feast of Shelters*
This reminded the people of their time in the desert. They built shelters of branches and lived in them for a week.

*The Passover and Feast of Unleavened Bread*
This celebrated the time when God rescued the people from Egypt, when God passed over them (that is, spared them).

*The Feast of Weeks or Harvest*
The Israelites offered God the first crops from their harvest, thanking God for all the crops.

## MOVING GOD'S TENT

When the Israelites moved on to a different place they took God's special tent with them.

It was all very organized. Everybody knew what they had to do.

The Levites were in charge of carrying the ark.

The Gershon family, under the direction of High Priest Aaron, had to carry all the coverings of the meeting tent. They were also responsible for folding up and transporting the curtains of the courtyard that surrounded the holy tent.

**So Moses took the wagons and the oxen, and gave them to the Levites.**

*Numbers 7:6*

# The Ten Commandments

108

Three months to the day after the Israelites left Egypt they arrived at the Desert of Sinai.

God called Moses to the top of Mount Sinai and there gave the Ten Commandments.

COMMANDMENTS ONE TO FOUR

1 "Do not have any other gods
   except for me."

2 "Do not make any idols."

3 "Do not misuse God's name."

4 "Keep the Sabbath as a holy day."

*Israel camped there [in
the wilderness of Sinai]
in front of the mountain.*

*Exodus 19:2*

COMMANDMENTS FIVE TO TEN

5 "Respect your parents."

6 "You must not murder anyone."

7 "You must not commit adultery."

8 "You must not steal."

9 "You must not tell lies about your neighbor in court."

10 "You must not want things that don't belong to you."

In the desert God continued to care for and look after the people. God gave them laws to live by, laws to help them.

God even made sure that slaves were protected from being mistreated by their masters. If a master knocked out a slave's tooth, the master had to free that slave.

*"If you heed these ordinances [laws], the Lord your God . . . will love you, bless you, and . . . the increase of your cattle and the issue of your flock."*

Deuteronomy 7:12,13

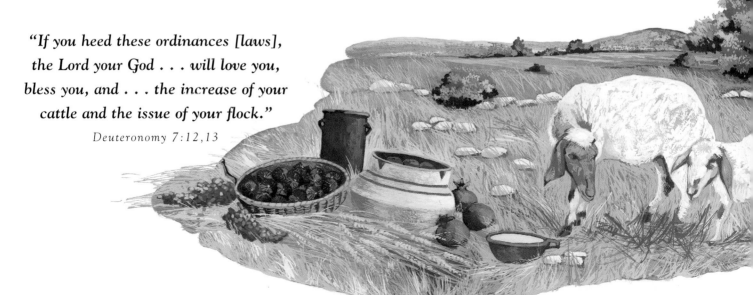

# Freedom and justice for all

110

## BE KIND TO EACH OTHER

God told Moses to tell the people to care for each other.

"Don't cheat one another.

"Don't be unkind to blind or deaf people.

"Look after people who don't have anyone to care for them.

"Always remember how you felt as slaves in Egypt, and treat others better."

## CARE FOR THE LAND

God also wanted people to take care of the land. "You may live on it, but it belongs to me," God explained.

Seven was a special number to remember. Every seventh year was to be a year of rest for the land — just as every seventh day of the week was a day of rest for the people. God said that in the seventh year people shouldn't plant seeds, plow, or cut down vines; but they could eat whatever grew naturally.

*You shall love the Lord your God with all your heart, and with all your soul, and with all your might.*

Deuteronomy 6:5

*You shall love your neighbor as yourself.*

Leviticus 19:18

*Then you shall . . . have the trumpet sounded throughout all your land. And you shall hallow the fiftieth year and you shall proclaim liberty throughout the land to all its inhabitants.*

*Leviticus 25:9-10*

## A HOLY YEAR

Every fifty years was a very holy year, a year of jubilee. A trumpet blast would announce that everyone was to be free from debt and slavery.

Sometimes people became so poor that they sold their land to pay debts. "On the fiftieth year, all the land goes back to its original owners," said God. Sometimes people had to sell their house to buy food. In the jubilee year, the houses must be given back. Sometimes people became so poor someone else had to pay their debts. "Don't make people slaves," said God. "On the fiftieth year all the debts must be forgiven. Set everyone free." This rule wasn't just for the Israelites, it was for everyone, even foreigners.

## IMPORTANT LAWS

The laws helped the women and men understand that they were people who followed God. Some laws became central to the life of the Jewish people. Two laws were quoted by Jesus as the greatest commandments (see above).

# Laws to live by

112

In the desert God gave Moses all kinds of laws. As well as religious laws there were laws about how to help foreigners and strangers and not to take revenge.

### LAWS ABOUT WHAT TO EAT

God knew that not all animals and plants were fit for humans to eat.

God said that the people were not to eat pigs. God knew what food would keep the people healthy and strong so God told them not to eat things like rats and lizards.

Some of the food laws were also religious laws. They helped the people to remember, in everyday ways like eating, that they were different and that they followed God and not the gods of other peoples around them.

*"You shall not do as they do in the land of Canaan, to which I am bringing you. You shall not follow their statutes . . . you shall keep my statutes."*

*Leviticus 18:3-4*

## Hebrew Scriptures

*Chapter 7: From the Bible books of Numbers, Judges and Samuel*

# The judges and Samson

## Introduction

*As they marched toward Canaan, the Israelites spread fear among their enemies. A talking donkey had to teach a foreign prophet a lesson.*

*The judges of Israel were both leaders, commanders-in-chief during times of war, and judges who settled arguments the Israelites had among themselves, during times of peace.*

*We are also introduced to Samuel who, when he was still a boy, heard God calling him in the night.*

*In these pages we meet the famous woman judge, Deborah, Jael and her tent peg and hammer, Gideon and his army which God told him to reduce from 32,000 to 300, and Samson and his bulging muscles.*

# Balaam's talking donkey

114

## THE PEOPLE OF MOAB ARE SCARED

On their way to the land of Canaan the Israelites had to pass close to the land of Moab, where Balak was the king. The people of Moab were terrified.

"Look, there are so many of them," said the people of Moab, shaking with fear. "This mob will take everything we have. They'd be like an ox eating up all the grass."

*The donkey saw the angel of God standing in the road . . . so the donkey turned off the road and went into the field.*

*Numbers 22:23*

## THE KING SENDS FOR BALAAM

"Go and get that prophet, Balaam," bellowed King Balak.

"He's a prophet," said Balak. "It's his job to curse people. We'll pay him lots of money and get him to put a curse on these people who've come up from Egypt."

## BALAAM HITS OUT AT HIS DONKEY

God didn't want Balaam to go and told him that, if he did go, he must say only what God told him.

Balaam set out riding his faithful donkey. Suddenly, the donkey saw an angel standing in the path. The angel had a drawn sword. If they moved forward, they would be killed on the spot.

So the donkey left the path and went into a field. Balaam lashed out at the donkey, hitting with a stick. "Get back on to the road," he yelled.

Later, the path narrowed as it went between two vineyards with a wall on each side. The donkey saw the angel again and bumped into one of the walls, hurting Balaam's foot. Balaam hit out at the poor donkey again.

# Balaam listens to the donkey

116

### THE TALKING DONKEY

The third time the angel appeared, the donkey just sat down. Balaam beat the donkey again. "Why have you hit me three times?" the donkey asked.

Balaam forgot that donkeys don't speak and replied, "You've made a fool of me. If only I had a sword to hand, I'd use that on you!"

The donkey carried on the conversation, "Have I ever acted like this before?"

"No," admitted Balaam, thoughtfully.

**When the donkey saw the angel of God, it scraped against the wall, and scraped Balaam's foot.**

Numbers 22:25

## BALAAM SEES THE ANGEL

When God saw that Balaam was willing to listen to a donkey and to admit that he may not be aware of everything that's going on, God let Balaam see the angel with the sword. Balaam fell to the ground and bowed low.

"I did wrong. I did not know you were standing in the road," explained Balaam.

## BALAAM DOES NOT CURSE THE ISRAELITES

By the time Balaam finished his journey he knew what God wanted him to say. His message to King Balak was, "I am telling you only what God tells me to say. God is with these people. They are as strong as a lioness. Anyone who blesses these people will be blessed. Anyone who curses these people will be cursed."

As a result of this, King Balak did not attack the Israelites.

# After Joshua

118

### Disobeying God

It was so sad. Despite everything Joshua had said — about obeying God and keeping God's laws — the Israelites started to worship the gods of the people who lived around them.

### God's action

God was angry with the people for disobeying. So God allowed the people to be robbed and defeated by their enemies.

### The people ask for God's help

Then the Israelites turned back to God in their hearts and cried out, "Oh, God, we're in such a mess. Save us from our enemies."

### Judges to the rescue

Then God chose people who were called "judges" to lead the Israelites. So long as God's people obeyed God they defeated their enemies.

## DEBORAH, THE JUDGE

Deborah, a prophet, was also a judge of the Israelites. Often as Deborah sat under her favorite palm tree, people brought their disagreements to her. If someone was accused of a crime, Deborah judged the case and decided what the wrongdoer must do to make amends.

## STOP SISERA'S ARMY

One day, Deborah sent for Barak. "God says you're to gather 10,000 men to fight Sisera," she said. Barak was scared. Sisera, a Canaanite general, was a powerful enemy. He had over 900 iron chariots. For twenty years, the people had suffered under his cruel hand.

"God has promised us help," Deborah assured him. "I'll go," Barak said nervously, "but only if you go with me."

Deborah agreed, but she had a warning for Barak. "You're not going to be the hero. Sisera will be defeated, but by a woman."

*She used to sit under the palm of Deborah . . . and the Israelites came up to her for judgment.*

Judges 4:5

# A brave woman

## Israel's judges

*The book of Judges*
The sixth book of the Bible is called the book of Judges. It records the lives of the people who led the Israelites after Joshua died, but before they had any kings to rule over them.

*Judges*
These judges were not exactly like the judges in our law courts today. It is true that Deborah acted like a modern judge and settled disputes between people who came to her.

But Deborah and the other judges were also like military leaders.

The Bible mentions 13 of these rulers, the most famous one being Samson.

Sisera was running away from Barak. He came to the tent of a brave woman named Jael. "Come in here and rest, my Lord," invited Jael. Sisera drank refreshing milk from Jael's leather bag and curled up in a blanket.

Jael drove a tent peg right through Sisera's head as he slept. He died without feeling a thing.

Then Deborah and Barak sang a hymn together.

"So perish all your enemies, O Lord! But may your friends be like the sun as it rises in its might."

And there was peace throughout the country for a very long time.

*Then the Israelites did what was evil in the sight of the Lord . . . and they abandoned the Lord, the God of their ancestors, who had brought them out of the land of Egypt; . . . and they provoked the Lord to anger . . . Whenever they marched out, the hand of the Lord was against them to bring misfortune, as the Lord had warned them and sworn to them; and they were in great distress. Then the Lord raised up judges, who delivered them out of the power of those who plundered them.*

*Judges 2:11-12, 14, 15-16*

# Strange maths

### GIDEON'S ARMY

When Gideon led God's people, the Midianites were their number one enemy.

But Gideon thought that he could defeat them. After all he now had 32,000 soldiers. Gideon couldn't believe his ears: "You've got too many men," God told him. "If you defeat the Midianites with that kind of strength, the Israelites will never stop boasting about their power."

### FROM 32,000 TO 10,000

So Gideon reluctantly told his troops, "Anyone who'd really rather be at home than fighting this war can leave." So 22,000 soldiers ran home. But that still left a fighting force that was 10,000-strong.

### FROM 10,000 TO 300

Next Gideon took his men to drink from a stream. Nearly all of them, 9,700 to be exact, knelt down and lapped the water up. But 300 men scooped up some water in their hands and drank the water from their cupped hands.

"Right," God informed Gideon, "I'm going to deliver you from the Midianites with just those 300 men."

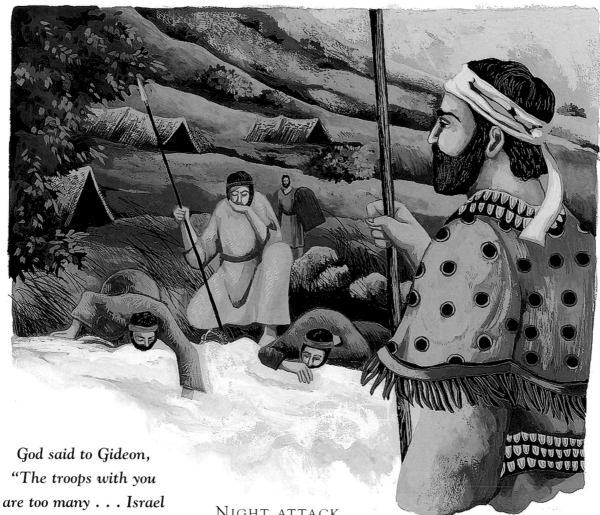

*God said to Gideon,
"The troops with you
are too many . . . Israel
would take the credit
away from me, saying,
'My own hand has
delivered me.'"*

Judges 7:2

## NIGHT ATTACK

In the middle of the night Gideon's faithful 300 men
surprised the mighty Midianite army with their
unexpected attack. The Midianites all panicked and
ran off.

# God calls a child

124

### HANNAH PRAYS FOR A BABY

Hannah knelt in the temple. Tears ran down her cheeks as she prayed, "God, if only you will give me a baby, then I promise that I will let the child serve in your temple."

Eli, the priest, thought Hannah was drunk until she told him how much she longed for a baby.

"Go in peace," said Eli, "God has heard you."

Hannah did have her baby, a wonderful little boy. She called him Samuel.

When Samuel was old enough, he went to work as a helper in the temple, just as Hannah had promised.

### GOD CALLS SAMUEL BY NAME

One night, when Samuel was still just a child, he was lying on his mat in the dark temple. He heard a voice calling, "Samuel, Samuel."

Samuel thought it was the old priest, Eli. "Here I am," he called. Eli woke up. "Go back to bed, I didn't call you," said Eli sleepily.

*God called,*
*"Samuel! Samuel!"*
*And he said,*
*"Here I am!"*
1 Samuel 3:4

It happened again, and once more Eli sent the boy back to bed.

The third time, Eli figured it out. "It's God calling you," he said, and he told Samuel what to do. The next time God called, Samuel was ready. "Speak God, for your servant is listening," he said.

## SAMUEL, THE TRUSTED PROPHET

Samuel grew up very close to God and became a wise prophet. All of God's people trusted Samuel. They knew when he spoke, that it was God's word they were hearing.

The times of the judges had been difficult. The people longed for a king — someone who would end the fighting in the land, someone who would bring them all together as one great nation.

They begged the prophet Samuel to ask God to give them a king. Samuel didn't think this was such a great idea. He talked it over with God many times. Finally, God helped Samuel choose a king for the Israelites.

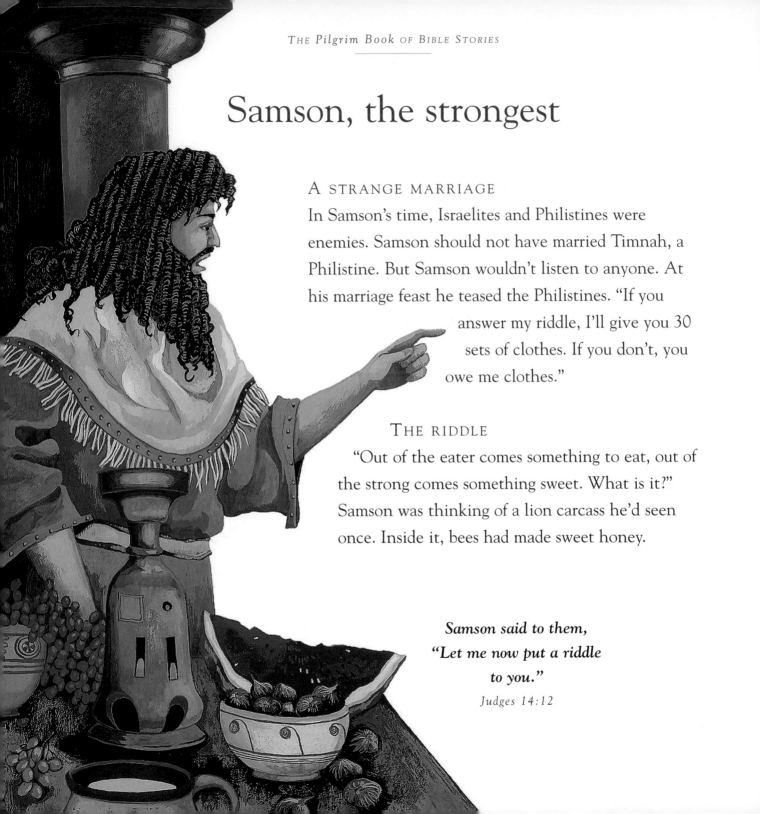

# Samson, the strongest

### A STRANGE MARRIAGE

In Samson's time, Israelites and Philistines were
enemies. Samson should not have married Timnah, a
Philistine. But Samson wouldn't listen to anyone. At
his marriage feast he teased the Philistines. "If you
answer my riddle, I'll give you 30
sets of clothes. If you don't, you
owe me clothes."

### THE RIDDLE

"Out of the eater comes something to eat, out of
the strong comes something sweet. What is it?"
Samson was thinking of a lion carcass he'd seen
once. Inside it, bees had made sweet honey.

*Samson said to them,*
*"Let me now put a riddle*
*to you."*

Judges 14:12

The Philistines didn't have a clue. But they forced Timnah to tell them.

### THE ANSWER

"What could be sweeter than honey? What could be stronger than a lion?" said the Philistines smugly. Samson boiled with rage, but he gave them the clothes.

### SAMSON, THE STRONG

Samson is very strong, but not very wise. He doesn't listen to his people and he drifts away from God. As biblical storytellers show, his pride gets in the way once too often, and the Philistines defeat him.

> *On the fourth day, they said to Samson's wife, "Coax your husband to explain the riddle to us."*
> *Judges 14:15*

# Samson defeated

128

Samson fell for Delilah, a beautiful but bad woman.
The Philistines longed to know the secret of Samson's
strength. They said to Delilah, "If you tell us why
Samson is so strong, we'll give you a whole sack of
silver."

"Samson," purred Delilah, "if you loved me, you'd tell
me the secret of your strength."

"Bind me with seven new bowstrings and I'll be weak
as a baby," lied Samson. Delilah tried that but Samson
broke them easily.

"Samson, my love, if you really, really loved me, you'd
tell me what makes you strong," Delilah persisted.

"Cut off my hair," said Samson. This was Samson's big
mistake. His long hair showed that he was supposed to
be dedicated to God, but Samson never took that
seriously. He never thought anyone could defeat him.
While Samson slept, Delilah called a man who cut off
his hair. He became weak and the Philistines
captured him.

*The lords of the Philistines
came to her [Delilah] and
said to her, "Coax him, and
find out what makes his
strength so great, and how
we may overpower him."*

Judges 16:5

## Hebrew Scriptures

*Chapter 8: From the Bible books of Ruth, 1 Samuel, 2 Samuel,
1 Kings and 2 Kings*

# David takes on Goliath

### Introduction

*This chapter opens with the tale of Ruth and her great loyalty. The story
starts with Ruth living in a foreign country with her mother-in-law, who does
not have a cent to her name. But the story ends with Ruth marrying one of
the richest men in Bethlehem. History also remembers Ruth for being King
David's grandmother.*

*In another exciting tale, David unexpectedly defeats the giant, Goliath.*

*The sad decline of Saul, Israel's first king, is eclipsed by the wonderful
reign of Israel's greatest king — David.*

*The queen of Sheba's spectacular visit to Solomon comes next.*

*A glimpse of the prophetic career of Elijah follows.*

*And finally, there is the story of an unnamed young slave girl who helps
a powerful army general find a cure for his leprosy.*

# The story of Ruth

### FAMINE STRIKES BETHLEHEM

There was a terrible famine in Israel. Naomi, her husband, and her two sons left their home in Bethlehem to find food. They traveled to the land of Moab, even though Moab and Israel were enemies.

In Moab, there lived a beautiful Moabite woman named Ruth. One of Naomi's sons married Ruth. But tragedy struck again. Naomi's husband and two sons died. Naomi had no one to support her.

"The famine is over, so I will go back home," Naomi decided.

### FAITHFUL RUTH

Ruth insisted on staying with Naomi, while Naomi's other daughter-in-law went back to her own home. Ruth said to Naomi, "Don't ask me to leave you. Don't beg me not to follow you. Every place you go, I will go. Every place you live, I will live. Your people will be my people. Your God will be my God."

### RUTH MEETS BOAZ

Naomi and Ruth had no money. So Ruth went out to a field to collect the grains of barley that had fallen to the ground during the harvest.

Boaz, the rich man who owned the field, strolled up at lunchtime. He'd heard how Ruth helped Naomi. He gave Ruth some lunch. Ruth was very surprised.

At the mealtime, Boaz said to her, "Come here and eat some of this bread . . ." She ate until she was satisfied, and she had some left over.

*Ruth 2:14*

# Boaz marries Ruth

*Now this was the custom: to confirm a transaction, one took off a sandal and gave it to the other.*

Ruth 4:7

132

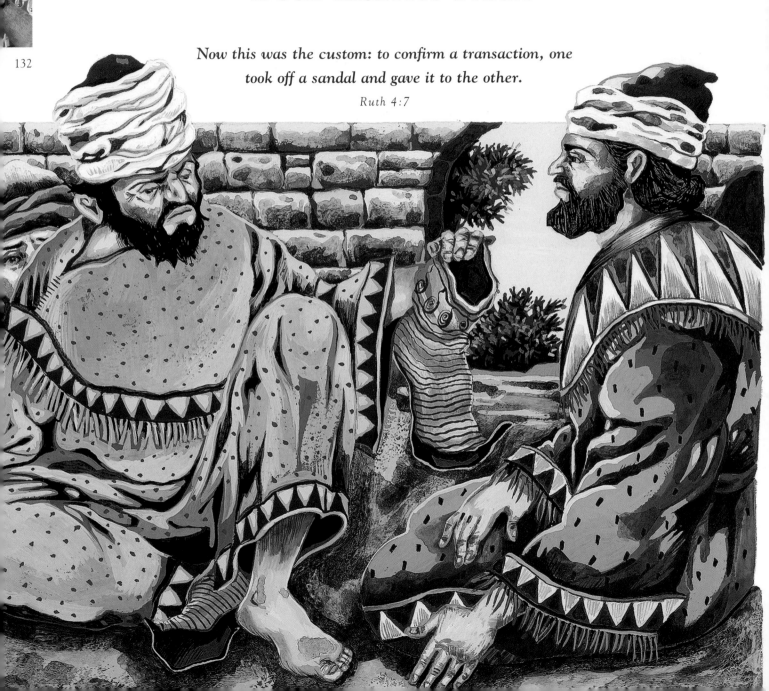

133

## Selling Naomi's land

*Naomi's land*
Naomi had to sell the land that had belonged to her dead husband. Women weren't allowed to own land in those days. The law said the closest relative must be given the first chance to buy the land, so that it stayed in the family.

*The town gate*
The place to do business was the town gate. Boaz went there with ten town leaders to help settle the matter.

*Boaz makes a deal*
Boaz was related to Naomi, but he wasn't the closest relative. And the closest relative wanted Naomi's land. "That means you'll have to take care of Ruth and Naomi," said Boaz. "No way!" said the relative, "I don't want the extra burden. You can have the land." He took off his sandal — a sign that he meant it.

*Then Naomi took the child and laid him in her bosom, and became his nurse.*
Ruth 4:16

Boaz was related to Naomi and Ruth.

He wanted to help them so he decided to buy the land that Naomi's husband had once owned. Then he married Ruth.

## GRANDMOTHER NAOMI

Naomi became the happiest grandmother in the world when a baby boy was born to Boaz and Ruth.

The baby's name was Obed. Obed had a famous grandson, the most famous king of Israel, King David.

134

# David takes on the giant

### A sling

David's sling was made from a small leather pouch into which a one-and-a-half-inch stone could fit snugly. This pouch was tied to two cords of rope, each two feet long. As the sling was whirled around, the stone stayed in the pouch. But as soon as one of the strings was released the stone would fly out with great force.

*Soldiers and slings*
Some soldiers were trained to be specialists in using slings. Such soldiers always hit their targets. "700 of these trained soldiers were left-handed. Each of these left-handed soldiers could sling a stone at a hare and not miss!"

*David and his sling*
Just because Goliath was a giant it looked as if David must be defeated. But David used his sling to protect his sheep by frightening off bears. Goliath did not stand a chance!

## GOLIATH ROARS

"What a lot of cowards you are," bellowed Goliath, the giant Philistine. "Who's going to fight me today?" he roared, as he waved his gigantic spear.

"Send one of your men to fight me," challenged the Philistine champion. "If he wins, the Philistines will be the servants to you Israelites. But if I win . . . hah, hah, hah!!" Goliath's words trailed off into a roar of menacing laughter.

*When the Philistine drew nearer to meet David, David ran quickly toward the battle line . . . David took out a stone, slung it, and . . .*

1 Samuel 17:48,49

*1 Samuel chapter 17*

135

## DAVID TRUSTS IN GOD

David stepped forward.

"I'll fight you, Goliath," the teenage shepherd said.

"You may well have a sword, a large spear and a small spear to help you. But I have the Lord of heaven's armies on my side. I trust in God," said David bravely.

"When I've defeated you," continued David, "everyone will know that God does not need swords and spears to save people."

## LET THE CONTEST BEGIN

David took out his trusted sling. He put in one of the five smooth stones he had just picked up from the river bed.

Whirl, wiz, splat.

The stone found its target — Goliath's forehead.

David killed the giant.

Against all the odds, Israel had beaten the Philistines.

*. . . struck the Philistine on his forehead; the stone sank into his forehead and he fell face down on the ground.*

*1 Samuel 17:49*

# Israel's first king

136

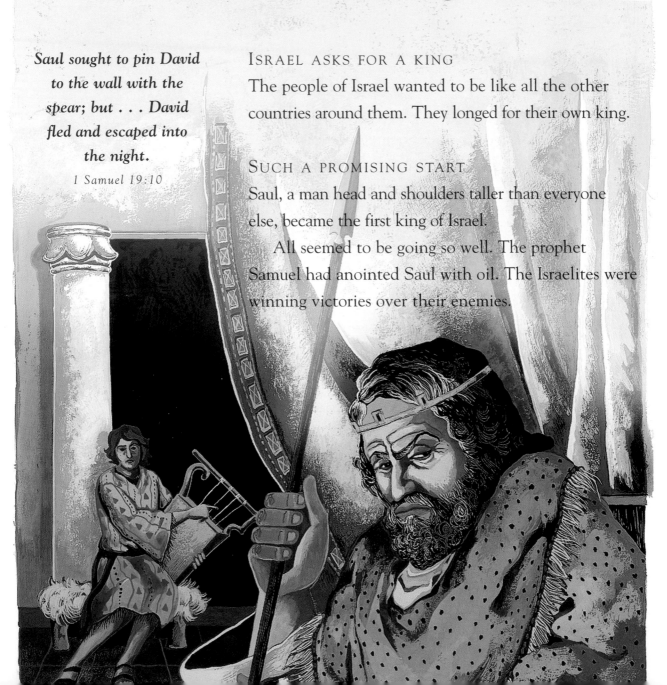

*Saul sought to pin David to the wall with the spear; but . . . David fled and escaped into the night.*

1 Samuel 19:10

## ISRAEL ASKS FOR A KING

The people of Israel wanted to be like all the other countries around them. They longed for their own king.

## SUCH A PROMISING START

Saul, a man head and shoulders taller than everyone else, became the first king of Israel.

All seemed to be going so well. The prophet Samuel had anointed Saul with oil. The Israelites were winning victories over their enemies.

**1 Samuel chapters 18, 19, 28 and 31**

## EATEN UP BY JEALOUSY

Saul often felt depressed. But he was soothed by David playing music on his harp.

But after David defeated Goliath, the people's favorite song rang in Saul's ears:

"Saul has killed thousands of his enemies.

But David has killed tens of thousands."

Saul was green with envy. He tried to kill David by pinning him to the wall with his spear.

Saul chased David all over the country, but David escaped each time.

## SUCH A SAD END

Saul was a broken man. He turned away from trusting in God. He broke the law by going to see a medium, that is someone who talked with spirits of dead people.

The next day the Philistines killed Saul's three sons in battle. When Saul saw that he had lost, he took his own sword, threw himself on it, and died.

*So Saul disguised himself and put on other clothes and . . . came to the woman by night.*

*1 Samuel 28:8*

# David: Israel's greatest king

138

### ISRAEL'S SECOND KING

After Saul's death, David became king of Israel.

David's army captured Jerusalem by climbing up the water tunnel and surprising the soldiers.

David made all the Israelites one great nation. He made Jerusalem the capital. And he brought the holy ark of God into the center of the city.

### GREAT WEAKNESS

David's greatness lay in his great love for God. But King David also had weaknesses.

He spotted the beautiful Bathsheba bathing herself. He wanted her. He was king. So he slept with her. As soon as David heard that Bathsheba

*It happened late one afternoon, when David rose from his couch and was walking about on the roof of the king's house, that he saw from the roof a woman bathing: the woman was very beautiful.*

2 Samuel 11:2

*2 Samuel chapter 11 verse 1 to chapter 12 verse 25, and 2 Samuel chapter 9*

was going to have his baby, he arranged for Bathsheba's husband, Uriah, to be killed in battle.

But David did tell God how sorry he was for taking someone else's wife, and for what amounted to murder. David prayed, "Have mercy on me, O God . . . cleanse me from my sin" (Psalm 51:1, 2).

## GREAT STRENGTH

David was great, not just because he won many battles but also because he was kind.

David asked Ziba, a servant from Saul's family, "Is anyone left in Saul's family?"

"One of Saul's grandsons is still alive," replied Ziba. "His name is Mephibosheth. He can barely walk."

Mephibosheth hobbled into King David's presence. He was afraid, because Saul had been David's enemy.

"Mephibosheth," declared David, "you and your family will always eat at my table."

Mephibosheth could hardly believe his ears.

*David said to him, "Do not be afraid, for I will show you kindness for the sake of your father, Jonathan."*

2 Samuel 9:7

READ-THE-STORY-FOR-YOURSELF

1 Kings chapter 10 verses 1 to 13

# King Solomon

## A ROYAL VISITOR

After King David died, his son Solomon became king. Solomon built a magnificent temple for God in Jerusalem.

One day Solomon had a special visitor, the Queen of Sheba. And she did not arrive empty-handed. The queen brought Solomon gifts: four tons of gold, spices, and jewels. Later, someone wrote, "No one since that time has brought more spices into Israel than the Queen of Sheba gave King Solomon."

## WISDOM

The queen of Sheba heard that Solomon was very wise, so she tested him with hard questions. Solomon answered brilliantly.

"God has given you this wisdom so that you can be a good and fair king," declared the queen. Then the queen of Sheba left for home with her endless line of camels.

*When the queen of Sheba heard of the fame of Solomon (fame due to the name of God), she came to test him with hard questions.*

1 Kings 10:1

# The dynamic duo

142

*Then [Elisha] set out
and followed Elijah, and
became his servant.*

1 Kings 19:21

### ELIJAH AND ELISHA

Many of the later kings of Israel disobeyed God. But
the worst one of all was King Ahab. With his equally
wicked wife, Jezebel, Ahab worshipped the so-called
god of the weather, Baal, instead of God.

At this time God sent two prophets to speak up for
God. Elijah was the senior prophet, and Elisha was his
assistant. Elisha took over when Elijah died.

### A DROUGHT

Elijah told King Ahab that God would bring a
drought. "There will be no rain or dew for the
next few years," predicted Elijah.

King Ahab was furious. All the

**1 Kings, chapters 17, 18 and 19**

*The jar of meal was not emptied, neither did the jug of oil fail, according to the word of God.*

1 Kings 17:16

prophets of Baal did their best to produce rain. But no rain came.

Later, just after Elijah said to the king, "A heavy rain is coming," it rained and rained and rained.

## ELIJAH AND THE WIDOW

During the drought, God told Elijah to go to the town of Zarephath. There, Elijah saw a poor widow gathering sticks. Hungry and thirsty from his long journey, he asked her for bread and water.

The woman sighed. "All I have is a handful of flour and a spoonful of oil. I was just going to bake one last loaf of bread. My son and I will have nothing to eat after that, so we'll certainly die."

Elijah looked her in the eyes. "Don't be afraid," he said. "Bake me a small loaf with what you have, and God will make sure you are never hungry."

The brave woman trusted God. She used her last bit of flour and oil to make a meal for Elijah.

A miracle happened! The woman's jars of oil and flour were never empty again.

# General Naaman's illness

144

General Naaman commanded the army of the king of Aram. He'd won victory after victory. But one thing made him desperately sad. He suffered from a dreaded skin disease. People said: "Don't go near Naaman. He's a leper!"

### A YOUNG GIRL

Naaman's wife had a young slave girl. She had been taken as a captive from Israel in one of the raids by the Arameans. She said to Naaman's wife, "I know a man from my country who could heal General Naaman."

So the general visited the prophet Elisha, and was told, "Go and wash in the river Jordan."

When Namaan did this he was cured. His skin became like that of a young child.

*[Naaman] came and stood before [Elisha] and said, "Now I know there is no God in all the earth except in Israel!"*

2 Kings 5:15

# Praising through problems

## INTRODUCTION

*This chapter starts with the book of Esther, which tells how a beautiful queen saved the Jews throughout the Persian Empire from a holocaust. The chapter then focuses on the sad plight of Job wallowing in a heap of ashes, beside himself with wounded pride and a body full of agonizing sores.*

*The book of Psalms follows. In the psalms all the feelings that we have ever had are there somewhere. The psalms are different kinds of prayers and songs. In the psalms there are prayers asking God for things and prayers thanking God for being so wonderful.*

*But there are also the kinds of prayers that we may not often dare pray. There are prayers telling God how fed up, or sad, or angry we feel.*

# Esther saves the Jews

## ESTHER BECOMES QUEEN

Long after Jerusalem was destroyed, the Jews who had been taken as captives were living in the cities of the Persian Empire. Esther was a beautiful young Jew. Her parents had died, so Esther was cared for by her uncle Mordecai.

One day, the king sent his servants to find the most beautiful woman in the land to be his queen. Esther was chosen. Before she left for the palace, Mordecai made her promise not to tell anyone that she was Jewish.

## A PLOT TO KILL THE JEWS

Haman was one of the king's top officials. Everyone bowed down to him—everyone, that is, except Mordecai. This made Haman furious. He planned a way to kill Mordecai.

Haman went to the king. "The Jews aren't obeying your laws," he lied.  He persuaded the king to sign a letter which would let Haman kill all the Jews in the Empire.

Uncle Mordecai told Esther of the plot. "Pray for me," said Esther. "I'll do what I can."

## ESTHER SPEAKS UP

Anyone who approached the king without being called could be killed. In spite of the danger, Esther went to the king and invited him to come to dinner with her.

Meanwhile, Haman built a gallows on which to hang Mordecai.

## ESTHER SAVES HER PEOPLE

The king came to eat at Esther's special dinner. He offered to give Esther anything she wanted. Esther told the king about Haman's plan to kill Mordecai and all the other Jews.

"I want you to save my people," she told the king. "That is my request."

The king was so shocked that he ordered Haman hanged on the very gallows he had made for Mordecai. The king sent out an order that the Jews should be spared.

The Jews held a great party to celebrate. "Esther has saved us!" they cheered.

*Then Esther said in reply to Mordecai . . . "I will go to the king, though it is against the law; and if I perish, I perish."*

Esther 4:15-16

# Job's suffering

148

*"My skin hardens, then
breaks out again."*

Job 7:5

### SATAN'S CHALLENGE

One day Satan, one of the heavenly beings, said to
God, "If you took away all the blessings you've given
to your servant Job, I bet he would curse you."

"We'll see about that," replied God. "Everything
Job has is in your power."

### SATAN ATTACKS

Satan was quick to act.

He killed off Job's 500 pairs of oxen,

he killed off Job's 500 donkeys,

he killed off Job's 7,000 sheep,

he killed off Job's 3,000 camels.

Then he killed off Job's sons and daughters.

### JOB'S SORES

Then Satan attacked Job. Job had painful sores all
over him, from the top of his head to the tips of his
toes. He tried to reduce his pain by scraping himself
with broken pieces of pottery. He was in a terrible state.

## JOB'S WIFE GIVES ADVICE

"Go on, Job," egged on Job's wife. "Be done with it.
Curse God and die."

"You shouldn't say such a thing," countered Job,
"we accept good things from God's hands. Shouldn't
we also accept trouble from God?"

## ADVISORS GALORE

Job was not short of other advice. One, two, three,
four friends came and told Job why he was in such a
mess. But none of them helped Job.

Job noted that wisdom was more valuable than
rubies, even though some people spend all their energy
digging up precious stones from mines.

*Miners put an end to
darkness, and search
out to the farthest
bound the ore in gloom
and deep darkness.*

Job 28:3

# Elihu's advice

*For to the snow God says,*
*"Fall on the earth."*

Job 37:6

At last, Job's first three friends stopped speaking.

At least Job's fourth friend, Elihu, had something positive to say:

"Look at God's greatness," suggested Elihu. "Look at the storm clouds, look at the rain, look at the snow. Think about the sun and its golden light. God is so wonderful. God is so powerful. God is never unkind."

## GOD'S ADVICE

Job begged God to explain why he was in so much pain. He heard God ask these questions:

"Who made the world? Who made the earth? Who made the sea?"

Job bowed his head.

"Will anyone argue with the all-powerful God and correct me?" continued God. "Look at this behemoth, this huge creature! Look at its bulging muscles. Look at how powerfully it can swim."

151

## Reading the book of Job

The 42 chapters of the book of Job can be a little confusing when they are read for the first time.

*Chapters 1 to 2*
These chapters tell how Satan attacks Job.

*Three comforters*
Job discusses his plight with three people who have been called "comforters" but who often give Job advice that is far from helpful.

Comforter No. 1 is Eliphaz (Job chapters 4-7; 15-17; 22-24).

Comforter No. 2 is Bildad (Job chapters 8-10; 18-19; 25).

Comforter No. 3 is Zophar (Job chapters 11-14; 20).

*A fourth friend*
Elihu adds in his more helpful suggestions in chapters 32-37.

*God's reply*
Job sees God's greatness in chapters 38-42.

**Look at Behemoth, which I made just as I made you.**

*Job 40:15*

## JOB WORSHIPS GOD

Job bowed his head even lower.

"Yes, God, I agree," said Job humbly. "Everything you do is wonderful."

God made Job better again, gave him a new family, and even more oxen, sheep and donkeys.

# Psalm 23

*God is my shepherd.*
*Psalm 23:1*

This is the most famous of the 150 psalms and is probably the best-known chapter in the Bible. One way of reading the psalm is to read it from the point of view of a sheep. Imagine that you are a sheep as you read it.

THE SHEEP'S PSALM

"God is my shepherd,
I shall not want.
He makes me lie down in green pastures;
he leads me beside still waters;
he restores my soul.
He leads me in right paths,
for his name's sake.
Even though I walk
through the darkest valley,
I fear no evil;
for you are with me;
your rod and your staff — they comfort me."
(NRSV)

## Looking at the details

There are many details in this psalm that should not be missed.

*"Green pasture" verse 2*
This stands for everything that makes you strong and healthy.

*"God leads me" verse 2*
Even today in the Middle East the shepherd does not drive sheep from behind, but leads them from the front, and they follow.

*"Calm water" verse 2*
Calm waters were a safe place for the sheep to drink.

*"Your rod and your staff comfort me" verse 4*
Sheep were often in danger of being attacked by bears and lions. A shepherd's rod, like a four-foot-long club, protected the sheep.

The shepherd's six-foot-tall staff guided the sheep and kept them from straying into danger.

153

# Thanking God for. . .

154

### GOD'S HELP

In Psalm 121 we can imagine the writer looking out over the fields toward the distant hills. They look so powerful and strong.

Then the psalmist remembers where human strength comes from. It is a gift from God.

God shelters you and keeps you safe.

He will protect you from all danger.

From now on he will keep guard over you

as you go out and in.

*I lift up my eyes to the hills — from where will my help come? My help comes from God, who made heaven and earth.*

Psalm 121:1-2

*May God be gracious to
us and bless us and
make God's face to shine
upon us.*

*Psalm 67:1*

OUR DAILY BREAD

The writer of Psalm 67 longs to receive God's blessing and God's kindness.

Then the writer recalls how much God is always blessing us, rescuing us from danger, and how much the whole world should give thanks to God.

God, be kind to us,

please bless us,

so that everyone will know how good you are,

how strong to save.

Let everyone praise you.

# Prayers for every kind of mood

156

### WHEN I AM SAD

Some of the psalms were probably written by King David.

When David prayed, he told God about his bad moods as well as his good moods.

Psalm 102 records the prayer of a person who is suffering. The psalmist does not try to hide sad feelings from God, but tells God how bad everything seems.

"God, I feel like that owl I saw the other day in the desert," says Psalm 102. "I am like an owl living in a wasteland. I can't sleep. I am like a lonely bird on a ruined house. I cry all the time.

"But," adds Psalm 102, "God, you are King forever."

*I am like an owl of the wilderness, like a little owl of the waste places.*

Psalm 102:6

GOD KNOWS EVERYTHING

In Psalm 139 David is cheered up when he remembers that God knows everything about him. He reminds himself that he was made by God.

"You know everything about me.

You know everything I think and do.

You made me when I was in my mother's body.

It's amazing — God, I praise you."

*For it was you who*
*formed my inward parts;*
*you knit me together in*
*my mother's womb.*

Psalm 139:13

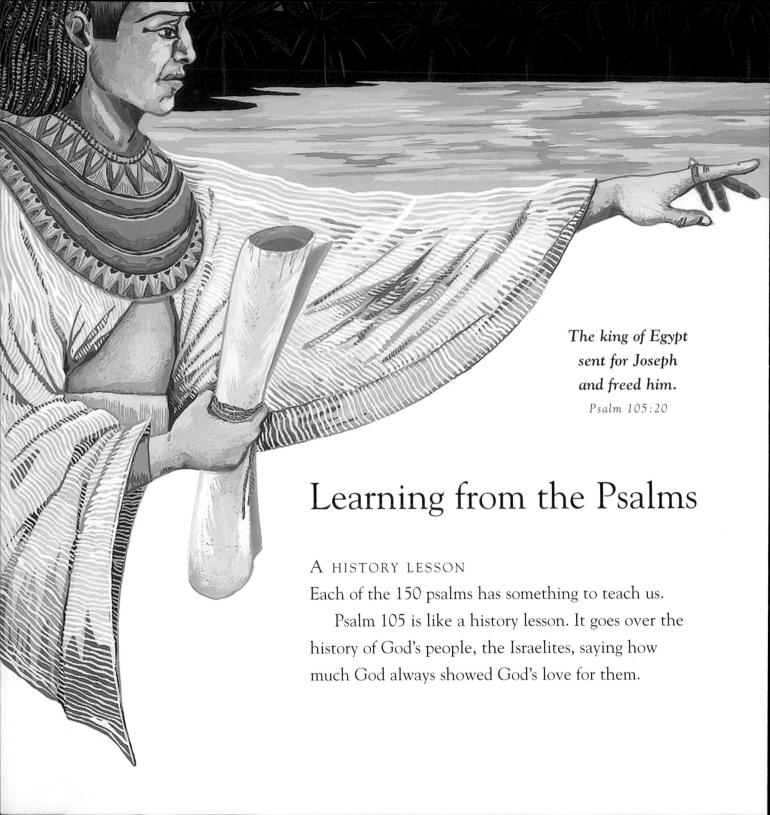

*The king of Egypt
sent for Joseph
and freed him.*
Psalm 105:20

# Learning from the Psalms

A HISTORY LESSON

Each of the 150 psalms has something to teach us.

Psalm 105 is like a history lesson. It goes over the history of God's people, the Israelites, saying how much God always showed God's love for them.

*Your word is a lamp to
my feet and a light to
my path.*

Psalm 119:105

159

JOSEPH

Do you remember Joseph?

"God called down famine.

There was no food in the land.

Then God sent a man on ahead of his people.

It was Joseph, who had been sold as a slave, heavy chains on his ankles, an iron collar round his neck.

But it happened, just as Joseph had said.

The king of Egypt set him free. The ruler of Egypt put Joseph in charge."

FINDING THE WAY

Psalm 119 is the longest psalm.

Its message is that God guides all who go through life following God's word.

# Songs of praise

160

MUSICAL INSTRUMENTS

The psalms are full of verses that tell us that we should praise God — that we should sing to God — that we should play instruments to make music for God.

Praise God with harps and pipes.

Praise him with loud cymbals.

Praise him with crashing cymbals.

Let everything that lives praise God.

Praise God!

**Praise God with tambourine and dance.**

Psalm 150:4

**Praise God with trumpet sound. Praise God with lute and harp.**

Psalm 150:3

## HEBREW SCRIPTURES

*Chapter 10: From the Bible books of Proverbs, Ecclesiastes, and the Song of Solomon*

# Stunning words of wisdom

### INTRODUCTION

*This chapter introduces us to a great biblical character, a woman named Wisdom, who is a central figure in the book of Proverbs. Proverbs is crammed full of advice on how to be wise. It was written especially for young people.*

*The book of Ecclesiastes follows. The big question this book asks is, "How can you be happy in life?" It mentions all kinds of things which do not bring deep happiness.*

*The next book, the Song of Solomon, is a book for people in love. It's a love song written by a king.*

# Proverbs galore

162

## WISDOM FOR YOUNG PEOPLE

If you like quotations, or wise sayings, or clever sounding one-liners, then the book of Proverbs is for you.

There is only one book in the Bible that was especially written for young people. It is the book of Proverbs.

## SOLOMON SPEAKS UP

The opening verses of the book of Proverbs introduce the book.

"The wise words of Solomon, child of David, king of Israel."

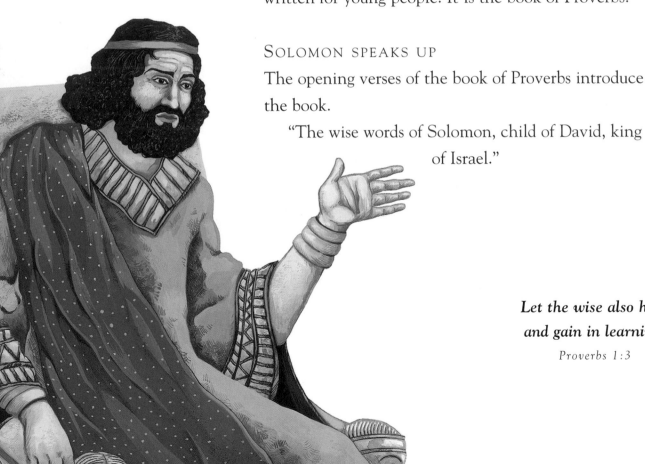

*Let the wise also hear and gain in learning.*

Proverbs 1:3

*Proverbs chapter 1 verses 1 to 7, and chapter 8 verses 1 to 14*

"These words will show you how to be wise.

They reveal the meaning of things.

Do you want to know what is honest and right and fair?

These words will tell you.

The 'don't-knows' will find they do know.

The 'too-young-to-know' will see the way.

Step one is being in awe of God."

## THE MOST VALUABLE THING IN THE WORLD

Wisdom is more valuable than the most precious jewels, more valuable than pearls, even more valuable than rubies.

*For wisdom is better than jewels, and all that you may desire cannot compare to her.*

*Proverbs 8:11*

164

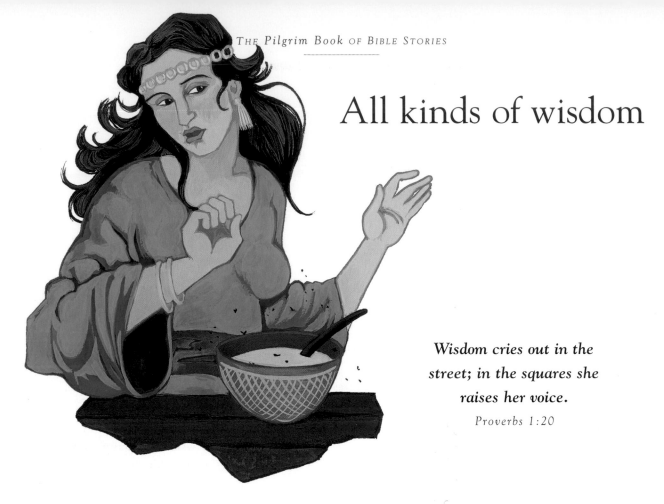

# All kinds of wisdom

*Wisdom cries out in the street; in the squares she raises her voice.*

Proverbs 1:20

## WISDOM IS CALLING

The book of Proverbs tells of a wise woman who was God's helper in creation. Her name is Wisdom.

Wisdom calls out from the busy street corner. "Pay attention. I have something important to tell you. Trust in God with all your heart," she says.

Wisdom sighs sadly. No one is listening. They prefer not to know. "What will you do when you get into difficulty?" Wisdom asks. "If you don't have me to help, you are going to be in big trouble."

*Proverbs chapter 1 verses 20 to 33, and chapter 10 verses 1 to 5*

*A child who sleeps in harvest brings shame.*

Proverbs 10:5

165

## LAZINESS NEVER PAYS

The book of Proverbs has many verses telling its readers not to be lazy.

"Lazy people have no money."

"A lazy person says, 'I can't go out, there's a lion in the street!'"

"A lazy person turns over and over in bed."

### Collected sayings

The sayings in the book of Proverbs were written by many unnamed sages. Solomon's name appears as an honorary author, because of his fabled wisdom. The sayings and proverbs were collected over many centuries. The book was finished about 500 years after Solomon died.

*Nation building*
"Doing what is right makes a nation great" (Proverbs 14:34).

*A soft answer*
"A gentle answer will calm a person's anger" (Proverbs 15:1).

# Nuggets of wisdom

166

## RESPECT YOUR PARENTS

Moms and dads are meant to teach everything that is good to their children. That's why the book of Proverbs says that children should follow the advice of their parents.

"Wise children are glad when their parents put them right."

*Hear, my child, your father's instruction, and do not reject your mother's teaching.*

Proverbs 1:8

### Proverbs from Proverbs

A number of the sayings in the book of Proverbs can be found in many books of quotations because they are so striking.

*A good name*
"A good name is more important than great riches" (Proverbs 22:1).

*A happy heart*
"A happy heart is like good medicine" (Proverbs 17:22).

*Starting right*
"Train a child how to live the right way. Then even when she is old, she will still live that way" (Proverbs 22:6).

*Tomorrow*
"Don't brag about what will happen tomorrow. You don't really know what will happen" (Proverbs 27:1).

## A super-mom and super-wife

In the last chapter of the book of Proverbs, chapter 31, there is a description of a mom who is creative, hard-working, and generous. She makes clothes for her family and is up at the crack of dawn to prepare the meals for each day.

In contrast to the idle person of Proverbs 26:15, this super-mom, "Looks well to the ways of her household, and does not eat the bread of idleness. Her children rise up and call her happy; her husband too, and he praises her" (Proverbs 31:27, 28 NRSV).

**The lazy person buries a hand in the dish, and is too tired to bring it back to the mouth.**

*Proverbs 26:15*

# Spot the difference

168

PLENTY OF FOOD

These two pictures may remind you of those puzzles which ask you to see how many differences you can find between the two pictures.

*Those who till their land will have plenty of food . . .*

Proverbs 12:11

## NO FOOD

169

The first picture is the result of hard work, which produces plenty of food.

The second picture is the result of no work, which produces no food.

The book of Proverbs also says:

Hard workers will become leaders.

Evil people want what other evil people have stolen.

**But those who follow worthless pursuits have no sense.**

*Proverbs 12:11*

# More helpful advice

### DON'T BE PROUD

Proverbs hits out against pride. It is not good to think you're better than others.

"It is not wise to brag, and show off and tell tall stories" (Proverbs 8:13).

"Proud people are always arguing; it's wise to ask for help" (Proverbs 13:10).

**When pride comes, then comes disgrace.**

*Proverbs 11:2*

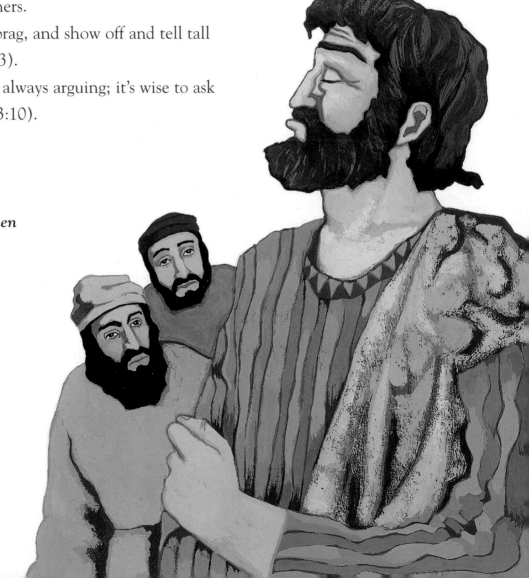

*Proverbs chapter 8 verse 13, chapter 11 verses 2 and 13, chapter 16 verse 28, and chapter 26 verse 20*

*The words of a whisperer are like delicious morsels.*

Proverbs 18:8

## DON'T GOSSIP

The book of Proverbs says that even though people like saying nasty things about others, to do so is wrong.

"A person who gossips can't be trusted to keep a secret" (Proverbs 11:13).

"People who gossip are trouble-makers who split up friends" (Proverbs 16:28).

"If there's no wood, a fire will go out; if there's no gossip, a quarrel will stop" (Proverbs 26:20).

# Self-control

TOO MUCH WINE

While some people think that there's nothing wrong with getting drunk, the book of Proverbs has a different view.

"Who always has problems?

Who is always getting into a fight?

Who is always moaning?

Who has bloodshot eyes?

Someone who sits up late drinking. The serious drinker!"

*Do not look at wine . . .*
*when it sparkles in*
*the cup.*

Proverbs 23:31

173

*Like a city breached,*
*without walls, is one*
*who lacks self-control.*

Proverbs 25:28

"Wine may slip smoothly down your throat, but it is poisonous, like a snake" (Proverbs 23:29-32).

## TEMPER, TEMPER

We all lose our temper sometimes. But the book of Proverbs says how good it is to keep ourselves under control.

"Patience is stronger than strength. It is better to control your temper than to capture a city" (Proverbs 16:32).

# What makes you happy?

174

WISDOM

Money and food do not bring happiness that lasts, says the book of Ecclesiastes. Only wisdom does that.

Wisdom keeps you safe. (Ecclesiastes 7:12)

Wisdom makes you strong. (Ecclesiastes 7:19)

*The lover of money
will not be satisfied
with money.*

*Ecclesiastes 5:10*

Ecclesiastes chapter 7 verses 1 to 29, and chapter 3 verses 1 to 7

# A time, a place for everything

175

There's a right time for everything:

" . . . a time to be born,

and a time to die;

a time to plant,

and a time to pull up what is planted;

a time to kill,

and a time to heal;

a time to break down,

and a time to build up;

a time to weep,

and a time to laugh;

a time to mourn,

and a time to dance . . .

a time to keep silence,

and a time to speak"

(Ecclesiastes 3:1-4, 7 NRSV).

**Go, eat your bread with enjoyment, and drink your wine with a merry heart.**

Ecclesiastes 9:7

# In love

176

## SOLOMON'S LOVE SONG

The Song of Solomon is a love song dedicated to King Solomon.

## MANY PICTURES

The song uses many images: My lover is like a gazelle, a wild dove, or a beautiful garden. Nothing can drown love.

"Love is strong as death,
passion fierce as the grave.
Its flashes are flashes of fire,
a raging flame.
Many waters cannot quench love,
neither can floods drown it"
(Song of Solomon 8:6-7 NRSV).

*Be like a gazelle or a young stag upon the mountains of spices!*

Song of Solomon 8:14

## HEBREW SCRIPTURES

*Chapter 11: From the Bible book of Isaiah*

# Isaiah's message of hope

INTRODUCTION

*The contrasting messages of Israel's greatest prophet, Isaiah, take up this whole chapter.*

*Isaiah's dire warnings about God's judgment seem hard.*

*But Isaiah had to deal with major problems: How could he shake such a proud people out of their complacency? How could he stop them relying on and worshiping their wooden idols? How could he stop them cheating and mistreating the poor?*

*Yet Isaiah also has many messages of hope.*

*He pictures a future time when the wolf and lamb will live together peacefully. He talks of a new city made of jewels and, best of all, a time of peace when God's people will be able to enjoy the fruit of their own gardens.*

# "Look out, Jerusalem!"

178

## TWO KINGDOMS

The country David and Solomon had ruled had split into two. The northern kingdom, called Israel, had been invaded by the Assyrians.

Isaiah, God's prophet, warns the southern kingdom, Judah, that the same thing will happen to them.

## PROUD PEOPLE

But the people had no time to listen.

"Come on," the rich people of Jerusalem said to each other, "let's strut around the town. And don't forget your jewelry, dazzling bracelets, and fancy robes."

"You cheat the poor to get rich," accused Isaiah. "You crush God's people, grinding their faces into the dirt."

*What do you mean by crushing my people, by grinding the face of the poor? says the God of hosts.*

Isaiah 3:15

*Isaiah chapter 3 verses 13 to 16, and chapter 5 verses 1 to 9*

# My vineyard

179

## THE SONG ABOUT THE VINEYARD

"Listen to my song about the vineyard," said Isaiah. "My friend who had a vineyard on a hill, did everything possible to get the best grapes.

"My friend planted the best grapevines and built a watchtower to protect the vineyard.

"But it only produced bad grapes.

"Now I'm going to destroy my vineyard."

Isaiah explained the song. "You people are the vineyard — God planted you. God expected justice, kindness and goodness, but all God hears is crying."

*God expected justice, but saw bloodshed; righteousness, but heard a cry!*

Isaiah 5:7

## Parables

Jesus wasn't the only person who told parables. Isaiah the prophet told a parable about vines.

*Vineyards*
Vineyards stood for God's people, the Israelites.

*Hills*
Vines were planted on hills so they had good drainage and so they caught the sun.

*Watchtower*
While the upper part of the tower was a lookout post to spy on enemies, the lower part was lived in during the harvest.

*Winepress*
This was a basin-shaped hole cut out of a rock. Workers would stomp on the grapes until the juice spilled out and collected in the hole.

# Remember Israel

THEY WERE WARNED

"God punished the people of Israel," reminded Isaiah, "because they cut themselves off from God through their evil."

"Evil is like a small fire," the prophet continued, "which starts off as a small bonfire, just burning weeds and thorns. Then it spreads and larger bushes catch alight. After that it turns into a forest fire as the trees catch fire. The whole forest goes up in a column of smoke. All the people will be burned up like that."

*Isaiah chapters 10 and 11*

*The cow and bear shall graze, their young shall lie down together.*

Isaiah 11:7

## HOPE FOR ISRAEL

Although Assyria did invade Israel, the prophet Isaiah looked forward to a time when God would bring peace.

"Then wolves will live with lambs.

And leopards will lie down with goats.

Calves, lions and young bulls will graze together.

And little children will lead them.

Cows and bears will eat together, and

their young will lie down together in peace.

Lions will eat straw like cattle."

*The light of Israel will become a fire, and God's Holy One a flame.*

Isaiah 10:17

# Other nations beware

182

## EGYPT

The prophet Isaiah did not restrict his warnings to Israel and Judah, where God's people lived. He also warned that God would punish other countries because of their evil. Even the super-power, Egypt, would suffer.

"The River Nile will dry up.
The river bed will be dust.
The canals will stink.
The ditches and streams of
Egypt will run dry.
All the reeds will rot,
and the grasses along the river
banks will wither"
(Isaiah 19:5-7).

*The waters of the Nile*
*will be dried up.*
Isaiah 19:5

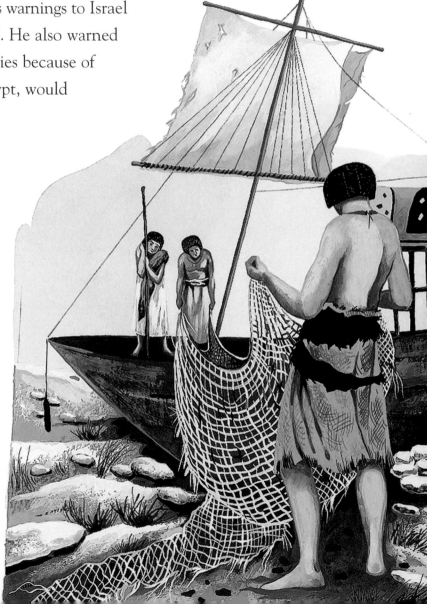

# Babylon

Another country which seemed to be all-powerful would also be defeated. The Babylonians did capture Jerusalem, but, said Isaiah, "God is even stronger than the mighty Babylonians."

"A lookout," predicted Isaiah, "will see men riding on chariots and horses, donkeys and camels. One of these cries out, 'Babylon is fallen. It has fallen!'"

### Babylon

*Babylon the mighty*
Babylon was Judah's enemy. The Babylonians later on surrounded and defeated Jerusalem and took the Jews off to Babylon into exile. Nobody could resist their armies.

*Prophecy against Babylon*
Yet Isaiah the prophet predicted the time when Babylon would itself be crushed.

God would break "the staff of the wicked, the scepter of rulers that struck down the peoples, that ruled the nations with unrelenting persecution" (Isaiah 14:5-6).

*Babylon did fall*
Babylon was indeed defeated on October 16, 539 B.C.E., when the Persian king, Cyrus, entered Babylon.

183

# "Don't be so proud!"

### THE POTTER

"Stop telling God what God should be doing," was Isaiah's message.

"Look at a potter who is in charge of a lump of clay. The potter makes whatever the potter likes with it.

"You Israelites are the clay. God is the potter. But you are telling the potter what to do. The pot is telling its maker, 'You don't know anything.'"

### DON'T TRUST ARMIES

Judah's leaders wanted to make a deal with Egypt.

"Their chariots and horses may look powerful," warned Isaiah, "but they won't save you."

Isaiah longed for people to stop trusting

*Shall the thing made say of its maker, "He did not make me?"*

Isaiah 29:16

**Isaiah chapter 29 verses 15 to 16, and chapter 31 verse 1 to chapter 32 verse 14**

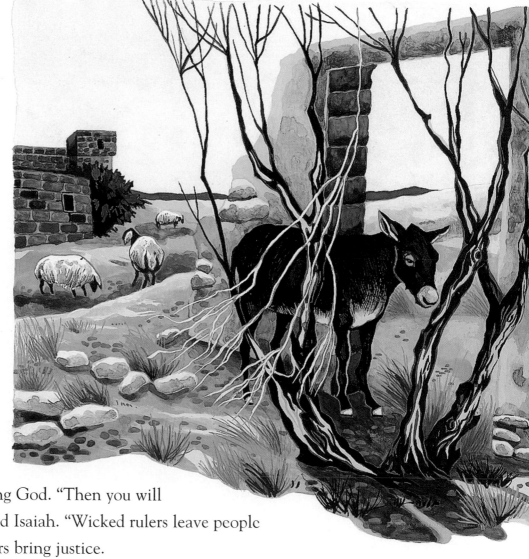

*"The palace will be forsaken, the populous city deserted."*

Isaiah 32:14

armies and start trusting God. "Then you will have good leaders," said Isaiah. "Wicked rulers leave people hungry but good leaders bring justice.

"If you don't listen, the palaces will be empty. Strong cities and towers will end up in ruins. Wild donkeys and sheep will graze there."

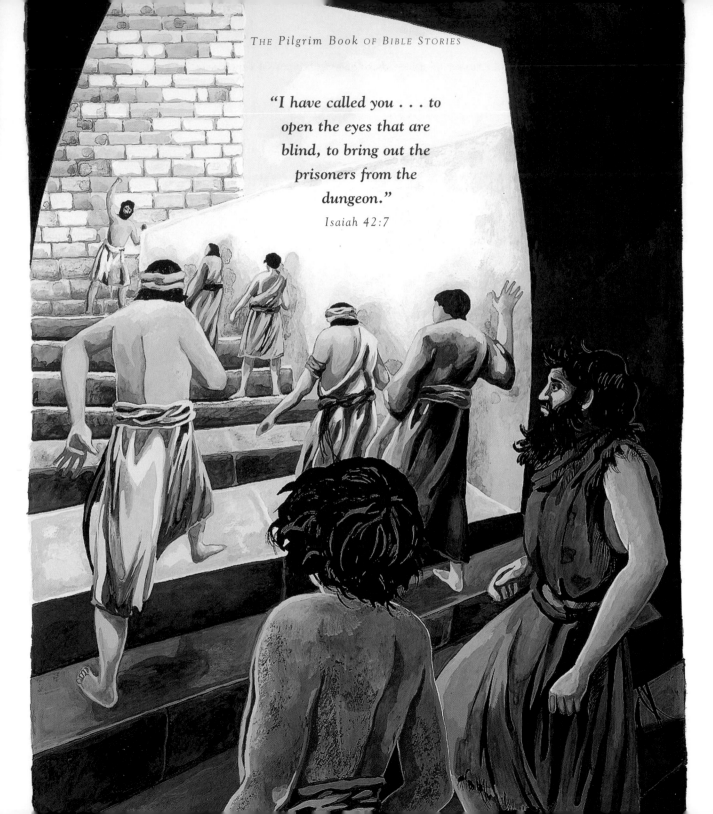

"I have called you . . . to open the eyes that are blind, to bring out the prisoners from the dungeon."

Isaiah 42:7

# Future hope

Isaiah told the people of Jerusalem that one day
God would send a very special messenger.

"God will do amazing things," enthused Isaiah.

"God will be a light for all the people.

God will help the blind to see.

God will set the prisoners free from prison.

God will lead those who live in darkness into light."

### THE CAUSE OF THE PROBLEM

Isaiah said that God's special messenger would not
allow idols to be worshiped in God's place.

"Can't you see," stormed Isaiah, "how useless idols are?"

"Think about it. Think how idols are made," reasoned Isaiah.

"You cut down a cedar, cypress or oak tree. Half the wood you
chop up for winter fires. Some of the wood is used for your oven
to bake bread. Then you take some of the wood, make an idol
and worship it. How crazy can you get?!" reasoned Isaiah.

"Can't you see how silly this is? You take wood from a tree,
use some of it to heat your home and bake your bread, then you
fall down and worship the rest of it," said Isaiah.

*Then he makes a god
and worships it.*

Isaiah 44:15

# Hope in days of disaster

188

## PROTECTION

"You trusted armies and idols and bad leaders more than God. You hurt the poor. And now terrible things are happening. But God has not forgotten you." This was Isaiah's message in a nutshell.

God still loved the people. God was going to send them a deliverer. This person would be like a razor-sharp arrowhead and would have great power to defeat any enemy. This deliverer would have great strength because the strength came from God.

## A NEW CITY

Isaiah gave God's people many messages of hope. Although he said Jerusalem would be destroyed, he painted a picture of a new city that God would give to the people.

"Jerusalem, storms have battered you,
and no one has comforted you.

*God made my mouth like a sharp sword, in the shadow of God's hand God hid me.*

*Isaiah 49:2*

Isaiah chapter 49, and chapter 54 verses 11 to 12

But I will rebuild you with precious stones.

Your foundations will be sapphires, rubies your towers.

I will use jewels to make your gates.

I will build your city wall from precious jewels."

*I will make your pinnacles of rubies, your gates of jewels.*

Isaiah 54:12

# No peace for the wicked

190

*But the wicked are like
the tossing sea that
cannot keep still.*

Isaiah 57:20

"God plans to bless you," said Isaiah excitedly. "He will give peace to everyone, far and near, and he will heal you."

"But," thundered Isaiah, "this is not the case for evil people. For evil people are like the restless, angry sea. Its waves toss up dirt and mud. 'There is no peace for evil people,' says my God."

Isaiah chapter 57 verses 14 to 21, and chapter 60 verses 1 to 5

*Lift up your eyes and*
*look around; they all*
*gather together.*

Isaiah 60:4

## FROM DARKNESS
## TO LIGHT

"Jerusalem is a doomed city,"
explained the faithful prophet,
"but one day it will be a blessed city."

"Jerusalem, rise up and shine
because your light has come.
The glory of God is shining on you.
Darkness will cover the earth.
Deep darkness will cover her people.
But the light of God will shine on you,
and people will see God's glory over you.
. . . Look around —
people are coming to you,
your sons and daughters from far away.
You will be filled with excitement and joy."

# Peace will dawn

192

God's people longed for peace. "Will we ever stop living in fear of our enemies?" they wondered.

Isaiah ended the book with this message of hope.

"I will make a new Jerusalem and it will be a city of peace and happiness.

There will be no more fear and crying.

Never again will enemies burn down your houses.

Your vineyards will be safe.

I will answer the prayers of my people."

***They shall plant
vineyards and eat
their fruit.***

Isaiah 65:21

# Jeremiah's prophesies

## INTRODUCTION

*This chapter is about Jeremiah, a prophet in Jerusalem who started preaching when he was a teenager.*

*God's people were under siege in the great city of Jerusalem. Food and water were running out. Outside the walls, the Babylonian army was preparing battering rams to crash into Jerusalem.*

*God gave Jeremiah a message for the rulers in Jerusalem: "Don't resist the king of Babylon; his army will destroy Jerusalem and take you as captives to Babylon."*

*Sharing this message made Jeremiah sound like a traitor. The rulers did everything they could to silence Jeremiah. His scroll was burned. He was put in prison. He was thrown into a well.*

*But Jeremiah's prophesies came true.*

*Then God's people remembered what else Jeremiah had prophesied — that God would return them to their homeland.*

# God calls Jeremiah

## TOUCHED BY GOD

God spoke to Jeremiah out of the blue one day, "Jeremiah, I have chosen you to be my prophet."

"You must be joking," protested Jeremiah. "I'm only a teenager."

"Don't say you aren't old enough," God replied, "I knew you when you were a lot younger. When you were

*"Now I have put my words into your mouth."*

Jeremiah 1:9

*Jeremiah chapter 1 verses 4 to 10, and chapter 7 verses 1 to 15*

*Do not oppress the
widow, the alien, and
the orphan.*

*Jeremiah 7:6*

still curled up inside your mother's womb, I decided that you would speak for me."

God touched Jeremiah on the lips. "See, I've put my words inside you," God said gently. "Don't be afraid. I'll be right there with you."

## JEREMIAH'S MESSAGE

"Jeremiah," said God, "go and stand at the gate of the temple. Here is the message you are to deliver."

Jeremiah obeyed. "Listen, people of Jerusalem, this is God's message.

"If you want to keep living in Jerusalem, change your lives. Stop lying and stealing. Stop cheating and hurting one another. Stop mistreating people who have no one to protect them. Take care of widows and foreigners and orphans.

"Don't listen to the people who say, 'We have God's temple. We have God's temple.' Saying that isn't going to save them. They must come back to God and do what's right."

# God warns Jerusalem

196

*"Are the birds of prey all around her?"*

*Jeremiah 12:9*

It wasn't as if God's people had not been warned. They had turned away from God. They now worshiped idols. Jeremiah said that God would bring them back to their senses by punishing them.

God said, "You will become like a bird that birds of prey attack. You will be attacked by wild animals. Shepherds will ruin your vineyards and trample on the plants in the fields."

## MORE TRAGEDY

The people of Jerusalem suffered a terrible drought.
There was no rain. The wells ran dry. They were
desperate for water.

Servants came back from the wells with empty jars.
The ground was dry and cracked and the farmers were
desperate. God's people turned back to God and said,
"God is our only hope."

"God is so sad about what is happening," said
Jeremiah. "He is crying like a parent who has
lost a child."

**"They come to the
cisterns, they find no
water, they return with
their vessels empty."**
*Jeremiah 14:3*

# The broken jar

198

Jeremiah was fed up. He'd never wanted to be a prophet in the first place. Now he was given a most unpopular message. And nobody took any notice of him.

God said to Jeremiah, "Buy a clay jar, and then while the people with you are watching, smash the jar into pieces. Then say this:

'The mighty God says: I will break this people and this city. Jerusalem will be just like this clay jar.

'I am about to bring disaster to this city and the villages around it because the people are stubborn and refuse to listen to what I say.'"

*"Then you shall*
*break the jug in*
*the sight of*
*those who go*
*with you."*
Jeremiah 19:10

*God showed me two
baskets of figs.*

Jeremiah 24:1

### Exiled

Jeremiah's prophecies about
God's people being taken off
from Jerusalem by their
conquerors proved true.

*605 B.C.E.*
Some people were carted off
by King Nebuchadnezzar in
605 B.C.E. See Daniel 1:1-2.

*597 B.C.E.*
Among the 10,000 prisoners
exiled in 597 B.C.E. were
the leaders, the craftspeople
and metal workers and all
the wealthy people of
Jerusalem. Only the poorest
people in the land were left.
See 2 Kings 24:14.

*586 B.C.E.*
In 586 B.C.E., the skilled
craftspeople who had
escaped exile in 597 B.C.E.,
along with some of the very
poor people, were rounded
up by King Nebuzaradan
and herded off to Babylon.

# Two baskets of figs

Jeremiah was given a vision by God. "Perhaps this will
wake up the people of Jerusalem," thought Jeremiah to
himself.

"I can see two baskets of figs," declared Jeremiah.
"One basket is full of lovely, ripe, juicy figs," Jeremiah
continued, "while the other basket is full of rotten figs
which nobody can eat."

"The good figs," explained God, "are the good
people. Although I will send the people of Judah out
of their country to Babylon, I will bring them back to
the land of Judah. I will not destroy them but will
plant them so they can grow. And they will want to
know me.

"But the bad figs," concluded God, "are King
Zedekiah and his advisors who still live in Jerusalem."

199

200

# Jeremiah's unpopular message

*Do not listen to them;
serve the king of Babylon
and live.*

*Jeremiah 27:17*

Everyone in Jerusalem hated the world's leading
superpower, the Babylonians. "So," the people of
Jerusalem reasoned, "it's Jeremiah's job to tell us
that God will deliver us from those dreadful
Babylonians. Why doesn't Jeremiah tell us that
God will work some miracle for us?"

Jeremiah put on a yoke of straps and poles on the back of his neck. Then
Jeremiah said to Zedekiah, king of Judah, who lived in Jerusalem.

"You must surrender to the king of Babylon and serve him. If you serve him and
his people, you will live. Don't listen to people who say differently — the false
prophets, the people who use magic to tell the future, those who say they can
interpret dreams, mediums and magicians."

## TAMBOURINES

Jeremiah delivered many messages of hope to God's people. In different ways Jeremiah said, "If you trust in God, God will bless you. This will be a time to bang your tambourines, to dance and to be joyful."

"The time is coming," says God,

"when I will make a new agreement

with the people of Israel and Judah.

I will put my teaching in their hearts

and minds.

They will all know me for themselves.

I will be their God,

and they will be my people.

I will forgive them for the

wrong things they did."

**Verses to note**

Apart from being Jeremiah's greatest prophecy, Jeremiah 31:31-34 is unique in two ways.

*Longest quotation*
Jeremiah 31:31-34 is the longest passage from the Hebrew Scriptures to be quoted in the New Testament. See Hebrews 8:8-12.

*A new covenant*
Verse 31 of Jeremiah chapter 31 speaks about a new agreement, or, new covenant. The name that is used for the second part of our Bible, the New Testament, is taken from this word "agreement," or, "covenant."

**Again you shall take
your tambourines and
go forth in the dance of
the merrymakers.**

*Jeremiah 31:4*

201

# Was Jeremiah a traitor?

### Jeremiah's scroll burned

God said to Jeremiah, "Take a scroll. Write on it everything that I have told you about Israel, Judah and the other nations."

"Baruch," Jeremiah called to his scribe, "I've got a big writing job for you." Baruch wrote all of Jeremiah's message in ink on a scroll. Jeremiah said, "Now take the scroll and read it in the temple."

"Your Majesty," said the king's officials, "Jeremiah has written a terrible scroll." King Jehoiakim ordered one of his officials, Jehudi, to read the scroll.

Jehudi began to read, but after he had read three or four columns, the king cut the columns off the scroll with a penknife. And threw them into the fire. Finally the whole scroll was burned.

Immediately, Jeremiah began to write a new scroll.

### Speaking out

Later, when Zedekiah was king of Judah, God told Jeremiah to take a message to the palace.

"What with all these unpatriotic words I'm supposed to say, people will think I'm a traitor," Jeremiah worried.

This was God's message to King Zedekiah:

"I will hand the city of Jerusalem over to the king of Babylon and he will burn it

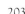

down. You will not escape from the army of Babylon. You will be caught and taken to Babylon as a captive."

King Zedekiah got so angry he ordered the palace guard to seize Jeremiah and keep him under lock and key.

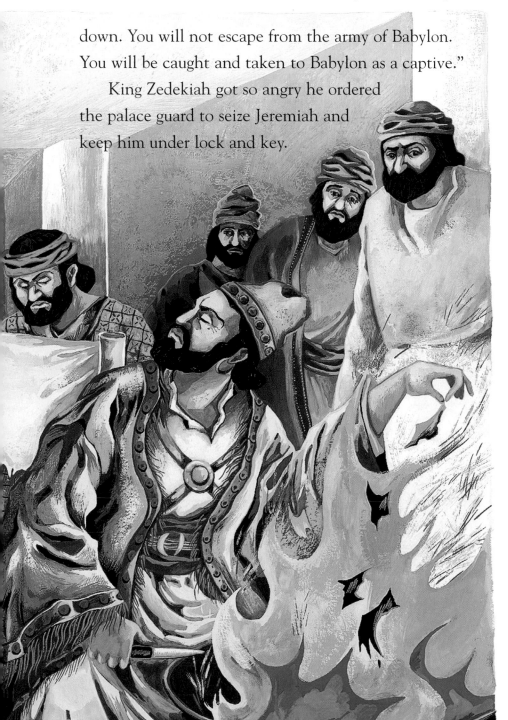

*As Jehudi read three or four columns, the king would cut them off with a penknife and throw them into the brazier.*

Jeremiah 36:23

## Ink

*Baruch used ink*
Baruch said, "I wrote down all the words with ink on this scroll"
(Jeremiah 36:18).

This is the only place in the Hebrew Scriptures where ink is mentioned.

*Making ink*
In Jeremiah's day, ink was made from soot or lampblack (a black colloidal substance made mostly of carbon). This was then mixed with arabic gum or oil.

# Into the well

204

## THE EGYPTIAN ARMY

The palace guards got so sick of Jeremiah's constant preaching they threw him into an empty well. The view from the bottom of the well was bleak. As Jeremiah shivered with cold and sank into the wet mud, he thought, "Is this where I'm going to be left to die?"

"All I did was to tell King Zedekiah what God told me to say: 'The army of the king of Egypt came to Jerusalem to help you against the Babylonian army. But the Egyptians will return to Egypt. Then the Babylonian army will defeat Jerusalem and burn it.'"

## GOOD OLD EBED-MELECH

Jeremiah's friend, Ebed-Melech, risked his own neck. He went to King Zedekiah, and bravely said: "Your majesty, Jeremiah the prophet has been thrown into a well. Soon he will die there. This is wrong."

*So they took Jeremiah and threw him into the cistern of Malchiah, the King's son*

*Jeremiah 38:6*

*Jeremiah chapter 38, and chapter 49 verses 7 to 22*

The king ordered Ebed-Melech to mount a rescue operation. With the help of 30 men and a lot of rope, Ebed-Melech hoisted Jeremiah to safety. Jeremiah thankfully breathed the fresh air. But he was still a prisoner of the court guard.

*"Although you make your nest as high as the eagle's, from there I will bring you down,"* says God.

Jeremiah 49:16

205

## A MESSAGE FOR EDOM

Jeremiah was given messages by God for other nations. Many of these nations hated the Israelites and attacked them. They thought that might was right and that they could get away with anything.

Edom was one of those nations. Its big problem was giant-sized pride. Jeremiah told Edom, "You can't escape from God."

"Edom, you've made a big mistake.
Your days as a bully are over.
You live in mountain caves,
and on cliff tops,
but even if you live as high up as an eagle,
God will bring you down!"

# There is still hope

206

*One runner runs to meet another, and one messenger to meet another.*

Jeremiah 51:31

Everybody in Jerusalem now knew that they were no match for the mighty armies of Babylon. But Jeremiah told them that this would not always be the case.

This is how Jeremiah put it, "This is what God says: 'I will send a fierce wind, which will destroy Babylon and the Babylonian people.'"

Jeremiah imagined the impossible: "One messenger follows another and each one tells the king of Babylon that his city has been taken."

# Jerusalem falls

The Babylonian army surrounded Jerusalem. They waited it out until there was no food left in the city. King Zedekiah and his army fled Jerusalem and tried to outrun the Babylonian army. But the Babylonian army chased them, and caught up with Zedekiah and his soldiers. Zedekiah was given a terrible punishment. The last thing he ever saw was his sons being killed before him. Then he was blinded. He was taken to Babylon in a bronze chain, like an animal. He was kept in prison there until he died.

With no army left to defend Jerusalem, the Babylonians walked into the city and burned it to the ground. The war was over — Jerusalem had fallen.

*The king of Babylon took him [Zedekiah] to Babylon, and put him in prison until the day of his death.*

Jeremiah 52:11

207

# Crying over Jerusalem

*All her people groan as they search for bread; they trade their treasures for food.*

Lamenations 1:11

**Lamenting over Jerusalem**

The city of Jerusalem was well defended and was difficult to capture because it was on a hill. But in 597 B.C.E. King Nebuchadnezzar and his Babylonian army besieged it.

In 586 B.C.E. they captured it. They tore down its temple and the city walls. The people were taken into exile. The treasures of the temple were plundered. Jerusalem lay in ruins for about fifty years.

The long book of Jeremiah is followed by a short book, called the book of Lamentations. It has five sad songs about Jerusalem.

Lines from the first lament record the plight of Jerusalem.

"The enemy has taken all her precious things.

Foreigners have invaded her Temple.

All of Jerusalem's people are moaning,

as they hunt for bread.

They trade their possessions for food so they can stay alive."

## HEBREW SCRIPTURES

*Chapter 13: From the Bible books of Ezekiel and Daniel*

# Daniel with the lions

INTRODUCTION

*This chapter includes some of the most amazing visions recorded in the Hebrew Scriptures.*

*God's prophet, Ezekiel, speaks to the Jews, God's people. They had been exiled to Babylon from Jerusalem, before the city was destroyed.*

*His striking visions of a caged lion, a crocodile, a valley of dry bones, and a rebuilt city of Jerusalem each carried its own special message.*

*Ezekiel taught the people that their much-loved city of Jerusalem had been destroyed because its leaders had turned away from God.*

*But these visions also gave the Jews hope as they languished in a strange land far from their city, their temple and, so it seemed, from their God.*

*Daniel was another sign of hope for the exiles. He and his three friends showed courage and faith: the friends in a blazing furnace and Daniel in a lions' den.*

# Model-making

### Seeing Jerusalem from Babylon

Ezekiel lived with some of God's people who had been taken away as captives to Babylon just before Jerusalem was captured. Through Ezekiel, God told the Jews that Jerusalem would be destroyed.

### A brick

God told Ezekiel to act out the siege of Jerusalem.

"Take a brick," God told Ezekiel. The obedient prophet soon understood.

"Draw a map of Jerusalem on the brick," God continued.

When Ezekiel was told to surround the city with an army, he used dozens of twigs and put them all around the brick.

Then he used many more twigs to represent the camps of the attacking army.

Then Ezekiel reached out for large, heavy logs. He put the logs next to the brick.

The Jews got the message. Jerusalem would be crushed.

### The sad people

"When the people of Jerusalem see their city being broken down, they will show how sad they are," God explained to Ezekiel. "They will replace their normal clothes with clothes made of rough cloth. Their bodies will shake with fear. Their faces will show how ashamed they are. Their hands will hang limply at their sides. Their voices will be like moaning doves. Their knees will wobble and give way under them."

## SILVER AND GOLD

Ezekiel was rather surprised when God then told him, "The people will throw all their gold and silver into the streets."

But then Ezekiel was quick to make the link between this gold and silver and the idols of gold and silver that the Jews made and worshiped.

"Your gold will be like so much rubbish," said God angrily. "You loved your beautiful jewelry, and you boasted about your golden idols. But you turned away from me. These evil people who are now attacking you will take all your treasured jewels and your gold and silver."

*"And you, O mortal, take a brick and set it before you. On it portray a city, Jerusalem."*

*Ezekiel 4:1*

# Acting it out

212

"My people are still not turning back to me and trusting me," God thought.

"Ezekiel," God commanded, "you're going to be an actor. That will make everything crystal clear to these rebellious people."

## DURING THE DAY

God gave Ezekiel stage directions, "As the people watch you, Ezekiel, you are to pack your bags during the day. Pack everything you need for an exile — as much as you can carry in one large sack."

*I did just as I was commanded. I brought out my baggage by day, as baggage for exile.*

Ezekiel 12:7

## DURING THE NIGHT

"As soon as it is dark," continued God, "make a hole in the wall of your house. Push down enough stones so that you can climb out through the gap with your things. Heave them up on your shoulder and walk out into the dark night."

## AN EMPTY LAND

"Ezekiel," commanded God, "tell my people: 'Because you have not obeyed me I will make the land empty and desolate. There will be no rivers, no juicy grapes to pick. It will be like a desert.'"

**And I will make the
land desolate.**

*Ezekiel 15:8*

### Ezekiel and the symbols

*The brick*
When Ezekiel used a clay tablet to represent the city of Jerusalem, he also took a sheet of iron and placed it between him and the brick. This showed that the siege of Jerusalem could not be broken.

*Food in a besieged city*
When Ezekiel was told to act out the siege of Jerusalem, he was told to store in a jar only the kind of food which would have been available in a besieged town: wheat, barley, beans, lentils, millet and spelt (Ezekiel 4:9).

*The broken wall*
When Ezekiel acted out an exile on the run from Jerusalem he dug through a wall. This was not the wall of Jerusalem, which was many feet thick, but the simple brick wall of his own house.

213

# Is God fair?

Ezekiel told many stories.

214

### THE FATHER
There were two men, a father and his son.

The father did what pleased God. He did not go up to the shrines of the idols in the mountains and worship them.

He was never unkind.

He never stole.

He shared his food with the hungry.

He gave clothes to those who didn't have any.

### THE SON
But his son went up to the shrines of the idols in the mountains and worshiped them.

He was often unkind.

He stole.

He mistreated the poor and the needy.

### "MY DAD IS GOOD"
It won't help the son to say that he'll be OK in God's sight just because his dad was a good person. God says that each person is responsible for what he or she does.

*He does not oppress anyone, but . . . gives his bread to the hungry.*

Ezekiel 18:7

*With hooks they put him [a strong lion] in a cage, and brought him to the king of Babylon.*

Ezekiel 19:9

# Two lion cubs

Ezekiel told a story of the greatest of beasts, the lion. This sad tale reminded people of what had happened to their great country and their kings.

215

## CUB NUMBER ONE

A lioness reared two cubs. The first cub became a strong lion that ate people. When the nations heard about the lion they dug a pit and put branches and leaves over it. The unsuspecting lion prowled around looking for the next meal, strode over the pit, and fell in. Then the lion was carted off to Egypt.

## CUB NUMBER TWO

The lioness brought up her second cub to eat people, too. No town was safe. When the lion roared all the people shook with fear.

But this lion was caught, trapped, and put into a cage. The lion was paraded before the king of Babylon. The lion's roar was never heard again.

**Lions and a lioness**

*Lioness*
The lioness (Ezekiel 19:1) stands for the countries of Judah and Israel. The lioness may also represent Jerusalem, which was thought of as a mother to the kings of Judah and Israel.

*The first cub*
The first cub may represent King Jehoahaz who was taken off to Egypt (see Jeremiah 22:10-12). Jehoahaz ruled Judah for three months.

*The second cub*
The second cub may stand for King Jehoiachin, who was exiled to Babylon when King Nebuchadnezzar captured Jerusalem.

# The great crocodile

216 Egypt thought of itself as one of the strongest nations in the world. But God had other ideas. God told Ezekiel to say that Egypt's days were numbered.

"You are like a great monster, like a mighty crocodile," God said about Egypt. "You are so proud," continued God , "that you dare to say: 'I made the River Nile. It is mine.'"

"I will drag you out of your rivers," warned God, "and feed you to the wild birds."

*"I am against you,
Pharaoh King of Egypt,
the great dragon
sprawling in the midst of
the channels saying, 'My
Nile is my own.'"*
*Ezekiel 29:3*

CRY OVER EGYPT

"Ezekiel," ordered God, "say this funeral song about the king of Egypt.

**This is who you are**

'You are like a young lion among the nations.

'You are like a crocodile in the seas.

'You splash round in your streams. And you stir up the waters with your feet. You make the rivers muddy.'"

**This is what will happen to you**

"Egypt won't be great forever," God assured Ezekiel. "Continue the funeral song:

'I will cast my net over you.
I will pull you up in my net
and throw you on the ground.
Your lights will go out.
Darkness will cover you.'"

*And I will cause all the
birds of the air to settle
on you.*

Ezekiel 32:4

# Two messages

*Someone who had
escaped from Jerusalem
came to me and said,
"The city has fallen."*

Ezekiel 33:21

### THE SAD MESSAGE

"Ezekiel, tell the people why Jerusalem fell into enemy hands," said God.

Ezekiel had been a captive in Babylon for nearly thirteen years. A person who had
escaped from Jerusalem came to him. "Jerusalem has been defeated," he told Ezekiel
in great distress, as he held his head with his hands.

Ezekiel told the sad news to the rest of the captives in Babylon. "It went all so
badly wrong for Jerusalem because her people listened to God's words with their ears
but disobeyed God in their hearts and lives," explained Ezekiel.

**Ezekiel chapter 33 verses 21 to 33, and chapter 36**

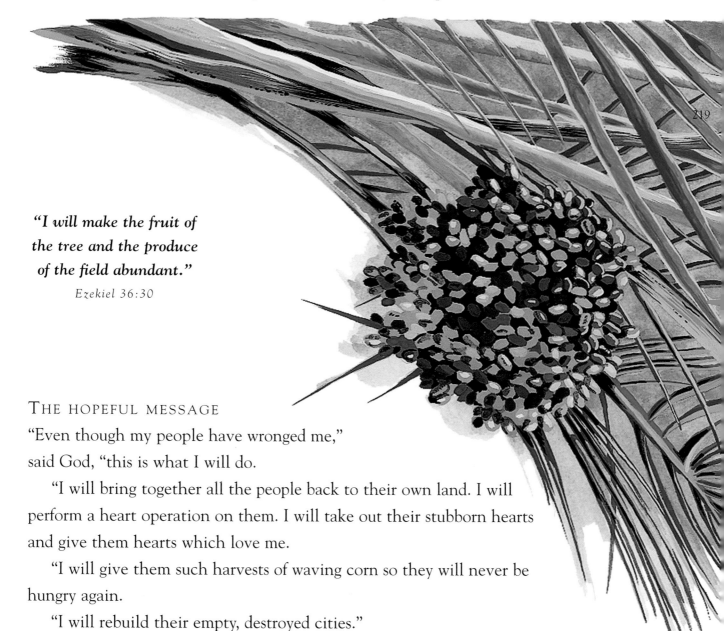

*"I will make the fruit of
the tree and the produce
of the field abundant."*

*Ezekiel 36:30*

THE HOPEFUL MESSAGE

"Even though my people have wronged me,"
said God, "this is what I will do.

"I will bring together all the people back to their own land. I will
perform a heart operation on them. I will take out their stubborn hearts
and give them hearts which love me.

"I will give them such harvests of waving corn so they will never be
hungry again.

"I will rebuild their empty, destroyed cities."

# Bones, bones, bones!

220

God gave me this mind-boggling vision. I just can't get it out of my mind. I was taken into the middle of a valley. As I looked around I gasped. It was full of bones. I could see ribs and skulls and all other parts of skeletons.

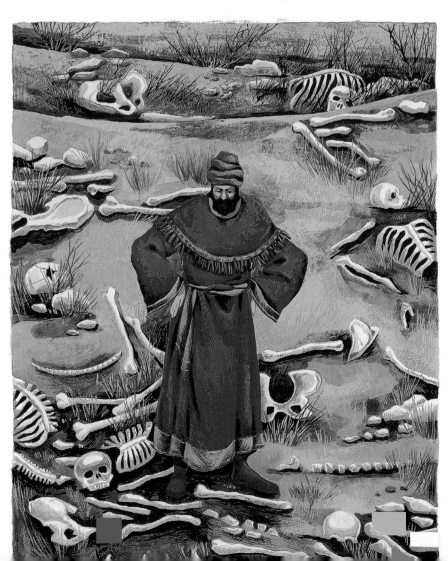

*The hand of God came upon me . . . and set me down in the middle of a valley; it was full of bones.*

Ezekiel 37:1

# Can bones come alive?

God asked me, "Can these dry bones live?"

Of course, I had no idea, only God knew that.

Then God said, "Prophecy to these bones. Tell them: 'Dry bones, I will breath into you. You will come alive. You will have muscles, and flesh and skin.'"

Then there was a deafening rattle as all the bones came together. The wind blew with hurricane force. And then I saw them — people, not bones — all standing up, like an army.

"That, Ezekiel," explained God, "is what it will be like when I put my Spirit to live inside people."

*And the name of the city from that time on shall be, God is there.*

*Ezekiel 48:35*

## THE CITY'S NEW NAME

"Ezekiel, this is how you are to end your prophecy," explained God. "Tell my people that I can see a new city of Jerusalem. It will replace the smashed city. It will have twelve new strong gates, each one named after one of the tribes of Israel.

"I will give the city a new name. I will be there, among my people, so it will be called, 'God is There.'"

everyone bowed down
and worshiped the statue.

Everyone, that is,
except for Daniel's friends
Shadrach, Meshach and
Abednego.

They wouldn't worship
anyone but God. So the king
had them thrown into a
blazing furnace.

## A FOURTH MYSTERIOUS FIGURE

King Nebuchadnezzar nearly fell off his throne when
he saw, not three, but four people in the blazing furnace.
"Look," exclaimed the King, "the four of them are walking
among the flames, but are not being reduced to ashes. And
look, the fourth one is like a god."

"Shadrach, Meshach and Abednego, come out of the
fire," commanded the perplexed king, "I see that the Most
High God, who you serve, has protected you."

King Nebuchadnezzar then made a new law: anyone who
insulted God would be punished.

*"But I see four men
unbound, walking in the
middle of the fire, and they
are not hurt."*

Daniel 3:25

# A night with the lions

224

Daniel served the king of Babylon well, but he was hated by some of the Babylonian leaders. "He's a foreigner," they grumbled to each other, "and insists on worshiping his own special god. . . If only we could get rid of him."

Then they caught him — he was on his knees praying to God through his open window, which faced Jerusalem.

*Then the king gave the command, and Daniel was brought and thrown into the den of lions.*

Daniel 6:16

They hauled Daniel before the king. "We've caught Daniel praying to someone other than you, your Majesty. So he must go into the lions' den," the court officials said, hardly able to hide their delight.

Reluctantly, the king had to agree. But that night God sent angels to shut the lions' mouths. So the lions did not eat Daniel for supper.

In the morning the king rushed to the den to see if Daniel was still alive. Servants hauled Daniel out, safe and well. Daniel had trusted God, and God had protected Daniel.

## HEBREW SCRIPTURES

### *Chapter 14: From the Bible books of Hosea, Amos, Micah, Jonah, Obadiah, Habakkuk, Zechariah and Malachi*

# Jonah's fishy tale

INTRODUCTION

*This chapter gives glimpses into the minor prophets of the Hebrew scriptures. Included are the famous Jonah, always a favorite, and Hosea, Amos, Micah, Obadiah, Habakkuk, Zechariah and Malachi.*

*Prophets used everyday things to teach God's people. There are weeds in Hosea, a lion in Amos, a high-flying eagle in Obadiah, plows in Micah, a strange stone in Zechariah, and grapes in Malachi.*

*Using these objects, the prophets taught people to be faithful and to trust God.*

*These prophets preached in three hard times: just before Babylon's army destroyed Jerusalem, while God's people were captives in Babylon, and as people went back to rebuild their ruined country. The prophets helped people understand why these things had happened and gave them hope.*

# Two messages from Hosea

*"Nettles shall possess
their precious things of
silver; thorns shall be in
their tents."*

Hosea 9:6

WEEDS

Hosea told the people of Israel, "Because
you have not trusted God, you will be
punished. You won't have enough grain to
feed yourselves. You won't have enough
wine to drink.

"Even if you are not killed, the
Egyptians will capture you.

"Your land will be a total disaster. It will
be overgrown with weeds. Your treasures of
silver will be taken over by weeds, and
thorns will overrun your tents."

**Hosea chapter 9 verses 1 to 9, and chapter 13 verses 1 to 3**

## IDOLS

Hosea tried to warn the people that terrible things would happen if they didn't start listening to and trusting God:

"You have sinned against God in terrible ways.

"You have made idols out of silver. Then you worshiped these idols instead of worshiping God.

"These idols may have looked beautiful to you because they were made by skilled artists, but in God's sight, they were hideous."

"You even pay more attention to these idols than you do to God.

"You show your love and respect for these idols by actually kissing them!"

### The Minor Prophets

The book of Hosea is the first of the last 12 books of the Hebrew Scriptures. These were first called "the minor prophets" in the late fourth century.

227

*The 12 prophetic books are:* Hosea, Joel, Amos, Obadiah, Jonah, Micah, Nahum, Habakkuk, Zephaniah, Haggai, Zechariah, and Malachi.

Before the birth of Jesus, these 12 books were joined together and known as "The Twelve."

They are called "minor" prophets, not because they are unimportant, but because they are so much shorter than the "major" prophecies of Isaiah, Jeremiah, and Ezekiel.

"The Twelve" have only 67 chapters in total, while the book of Isaiah alone has 66 chapters.

*They . . . make a cast image for themselves, idols of silver made according to their understanding.*

Hosea 13:2

# Insects invade

228

## VARIETIES OF LOCUSTS

Joel pictures the land of Judah being invaded by a massive invasion of locusts:

> "What one swarm has not eaten,
> another swarm has eaten.
> Locusts have destroyed the crops.
> Nothing is left."

## LIKE AN ARMY

Joel continues:

> "An army has come into my land
> with soldiers too many to count.
> It has teeth like a lion,
> and fangs like a lioness.
> It has eaten my vines,
> and destroyed my fig trees.
> It has stripped the bark off my trees,
> leaving the branches white."

## Locusts

*Their appetite*

The books of Joel, Amos, and Nahum all mention locusts. They are seen as God punishing people and are given as a warning, to help people return to God.

Locusts, a large variety of grasshopper, often collect together and move around in a million-strong swarm.

They eat every kind of vegetation they can get their teeth into. They can strip fields, trees and grasslands with devastating results.

*Their method of travel*

Some locusts fly like gliders. They use their wings to launch themselves into the sky and then allow the wind to carry them along. They can fly, or sail along, like this for up to 100 miles.

At night, they land in trees or grasses. All night long they gobble up all the plant life. In the morning they take off again.

Because of the great destruction they caused, the Romans called locusts, "burners of the land."

LOOK AT THE LAND

Joel then speaks about the farmers:

>"The fields are bare.
>The ground is sad
>because the grain is destroyed,
>and the grapes are dried up,
>and there are no olives.
>Cry out, you farmers.
>Cry loudly, you who grow grapes.
>Cry for the lost wheat and the barley.
>Mourn for the missing crops."

*What the cutting
locusts have not eaten,
the swarming locusts
have eaten.*

Joel 1:4

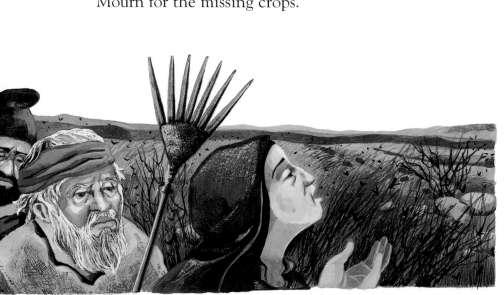

*Be sad, farmers.
Cry loudly, you who
grow grapes.*

Joel 1:11

# Amos speaks up against Israel

230

*The lion has roared!*

Amos 3:8

## THE LION'S ROAR

God's prophet, Amos, a shepherd from Tekoa in Judah, spoke against the people who lived in the country of Israel.

"Don't you know what it means when you hear the lion's roar?" he asked God's people who were not trusting in God. "It means that he has sprung on his prey," continued Amos, "he has caught his next meal. God's voice of judgment on your sins is like that."

*God said to me, "Amos, what do you see?" And I said, "A plumb line."*

Amos 7:8

## THE PLUMB LINE

"You are meant to be God's faithful people, built like a straight building," boomed Amos. "But God's plumb line will show how crooked you are."

## A plumb line

*Why it is used*
A plumb line has been used by builders since ancient times to make sure that the wall which they are building goes straight up.

*How it was made*
The plumb line had three parts. At the base was a lead weight in the shape of an upside-down cone.

At the top was a wooden rod, the same width as the cone. The weight and rod were linked by a cord.

*How it is used*
A builder places the wooden rod against the top edge of the top level of stones or bricks of the wall. If the wall is upright and true, the side of the lead weight just touches the lowest line of bricks.

**Alas for those who lie on beds of ivory, and lounge on their couches.**

Amos 6:4

LET JUSTICE ROLL

Amos spoke out against those who were unfair to the poor. "God says, 'I hate your extravagant worship and noisy hymns. Instead, let justice roll down like a river that never runs dry.'"

Amos criticized people who lived in the lap of luxury but didn't care what was happening to their country. "You think nothing can harm you," Amos protested. "You loll about on expensive couches feasting on the finest food and drink. And you forget about God."

231

# Jonah is rescued

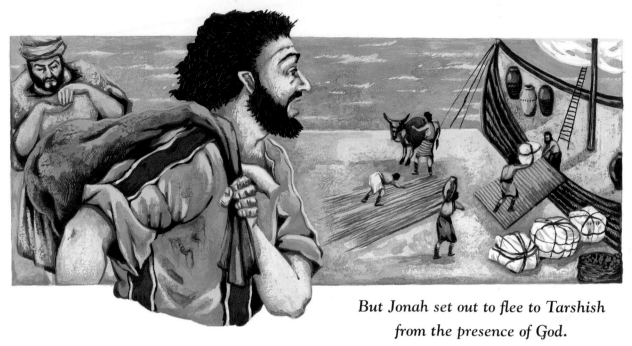

**But Jonah set out to flee to Tarshish from the presence of God.**

*Jonah 1:3*

Jonah did not like God's idea of going to and preaching to the wicked people of Nineveh. So he went off in the opposite direction and caught a boat to Tarshish.

But Jonah soon learned that it was not that easy to escape from carrying out God's orders.

"We're about to sink," yelled the desperate captain of the ship. "Quick, before the forty foot waves sink the boat, throw our precious cargo overboard." "That will make the boat lighter and help us to keep afloat," thought the experienced sailor.

233

## JONAH WAKES UP

The captain found that Jonah had been asleep all this time. "Get up, and pray to your God," shouted the captain in Jonah's ear as he shook him.

Jonah confessed that this storm came because he was running away from God.

## THE RESCUE

Reluctantly, the sailors threw Jonah overboard, as he had suggested.

At once the sea went calm, the wind died down and the rain stopped.

The tough sailors rubbed their eyes in disbelief. The largest fish they had ever seen swam along, opened its mouth, and swallowed Jonah whole.

Inside the massive fish's stomach Jonah thanked God that he had been rescued. Three days later the fished coughed him up, just by some dry land, safe and sound, but very smelly.

*Then God spoke to the fish, and it spewed Jonah out upon the dry land.*
Jonah 2:10

*Micah chapter 3 verses 1 to chapter 4 verse 5, and chapter 6 verses 6 to 8*

# Micah and war

### WARNING FOR LEADERS

"You leaders and rich people crush the poor," said the prophet Micah. "You lie and cheat."

"Rich people bribe the judges to get their own way," he continued. "That isn't justice!"

"As for you prophets," Micah raged, "if people pay you, you tell them what they want to hear. That isn't speaking God's truth!"

### PEACE WILL COME

Micah knew his nation was in big trouble. But he also knew someday there would be peace. "The time will come when we won't have wars to settle our arguments. God will help countries make peace treaties. People won't need weapons; they will make plows out of their swords and gardening tools from their spears. No one will be taught how to fight. Everyone will sit free of fear under their grape vines.

### WHAT DOES GOD WANT?

The people who heard Micah wondered what to do. "If we have a nice worship service, maybe God will be pleased," they said.

"No," said Micah. "This is what God wants, only this: do justice, love tenderly, and walk humbly with God."

But they shall all sit
under their own vines
and under their own fig
trees no one shall make
them afraid.

*Micah 4:4*

# Habakkuk's question

236

"Why," Habakkuk asked God, "does all the evil the people of Judah are doing go unpunished?"

## God's answer

"They will be punished," God replied.

"This is what will happen," explained God. "The Babylonians will punish Judah.

They are fierce and cruel.

Their horses are faster than leopards and more deadly than wolves at night."

*"Their horses are faster than leopards."*

Habakkuk 1:8

*Habakkuk chapter 1 verses 1 to 8, and chapter 3 verses 1 to 19*

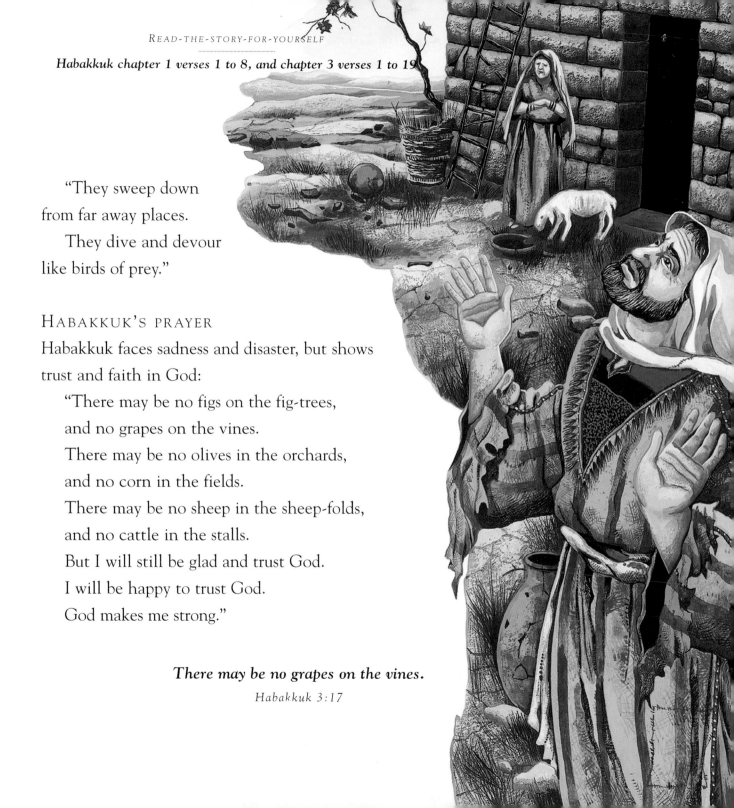

"They sweep down
from far away places.
They dive and devour
like birds of prey."

HABAKKUK'S PRAYER
Habakkuk faces sadness and disaster, but shows
trust and faith in God:
"There may be no figs on the fig-trees,
and no grapes on the vines.
There may be no olives in the orchards,
and no corn in the fields.
There may be no sheep in the sheep-folds,
and no cattle in the stalls.
But I will still be glad and trust God.
I will be happy to trust God.
God makes me strong."

**There may be no grapes on the vines.**
*Habakkuk 3:17*

# Zechariah's vision of a stone

238

God gave Zechariah a vivid vision to show how God would forgive the people of Israel.

"I saw Joshua, in my vision," recounted Zechariah. "He was all dressed-up in dirty clothes. 'Take off your filthy clothes, Joshua,' an angel ordered. 'See,' explained the angel, 'I have taken away your sin. Now put on these new clothes I am giving you. And put a clean turban on your head.'

"'I am now placing a special stone in front of you,' continued the angel. 'It has seven sides with a special message written on it. In one day I will take away the sin of this land.'

"'This is how I will bless you,' promised the angel. 'When the time comes, each of you will invite your neighbor to join you. And you will sit together under your vine and fig tree.'"

*"For on the stone that I have set before Joshua, on a single stone with seven facets . . . ."*

Zechariah 3:9

**Zechariah chapter 3 verses 1 to 10, and chapter 8 verses 1 to 23**

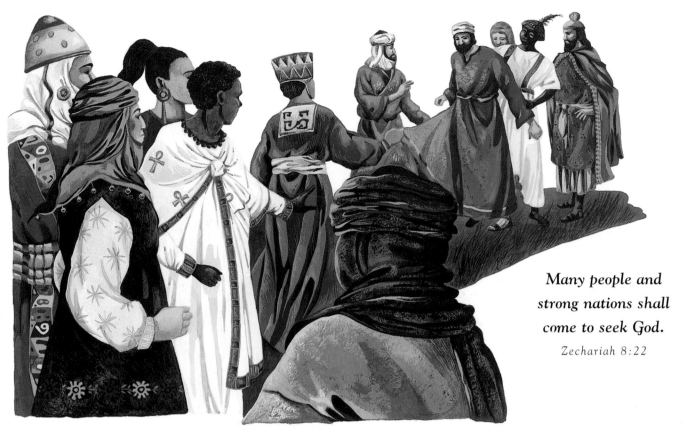

239

*Many people and
strong nations shall
come to seek God.*

Zechariah 8:22

## GOD'S BLESSING SPREADS

Zechariah predicted the time when many people from powerful nations would go to
Jerusalem. This time it would not be to capture the city, but to be blessed by God.

"This is what God says," Zechariah continued:

"When it happens, people will come from many different countries, speaking
many different languages. They will grab the Jews by the coattail and beg, 'Take us
with you. We know God is with you.'"

*Malachi chapter 3 verses 6 to 12*

# Blessed by God

Malachi, in the last book in the Hebrew Scriptures, looks
forward to the time when God will bless God's people. By this
time, many of the Jews had gone back to live in Jerusalem.

"OK, people of Judah," started Malachi, "I know that
you have rebuilt God's
temple.

240

> *"I will . . . open the
> windows of heaven for
> you and pour down for
> you an overflowing
> blessing."*
>
> Malachi 3:10

But you should be sharing more of what you
have — you should give 10 percent of your
income. Here is God's promise to you, if you
do this: 'I will open the windows of heaven and
pour out overflowing blessings. Insects will no longer
devour your crops. Your vines will be heavy with grapes.'"

# NEW TESTAMENT

*Chapter 15: From the Bible books of Matthew, Mark and Luke*

# Jesus the healer

## INTRODUCTION

*This first chapter from the New Testament is all about the life of Jesus.*

*It starts with stories about Jesus' birth and childhood. It then moves on to the time when Jesus was about 30 years old. Jesus chose some special helpers. Large crowds of people came to listen to Jesus' stories, such as the parables of the farmer and the seed, which were remembered long after he told them.*

*Jesus became a powerful healer of adults as well as children. He healed a man with a crippled hand. He also brought a 12-year-old girl back to life.*

*We are introduced to two very different sisters, Mary and Martha, and to other followers and friends of Jesus.*

*This book ends with the story about the day that Jesus' face shone like the sun.*

**When Elizabeth heard Mary's greeting, the child leaped in her womb. And Elizabeth was filled with the Holy Spirit.**

Luke 1:41

# Two babies to be born

### A SURPRISE BABY

Mary had no idea that she was going to be Jesus' mom until an angel said to her, "Don't be afraid, Mary, because God is pleased with you. Listen! You will give birth to a son, and you will name him Jesus."

### ELIZABETH'S BABY

Mary visited her relative Elizabeth, who was expecting a baby. "My baby's going to be a miracle baby, Mary," Elizabeth explained. "I am so old. Only God could give me a baby at my time of life."

### MARY'S BABY

Mary had astonishing news of her own. "Elizabeth, I'm going to have a baby too," Mary said joyfully. "He will be called Child of the Most High and Child of God. He is going to be a holy baby."

*Luke chapter 1 verse 5 to chapter 2 verse 20*

# Jesus is born

MARY'S SONG

Mary sang about what God had done:

"My spirit dances; God is magnificent,

God cares deeply about people the world
doesn't see.

God strengthens the weak and gentles the
strong,

lifts up the little ones, humbles the proud,

fills the hungry and sends the rich away empty."

A HUMBLE BIRTH

Mary and Joseph arrived in Bethlehem just before
Jesus' birth. But there were no rooms left in the
inn. So Jesus was born in a stable. Joseph put clean
straw in a box where animals are fed and Mary
gently placed the new-born baby Jesus on the straw.

That night, angels told the news about the birth
to shepherds up in the hills. "Glory to God and
peace on earth," sang the angels. The shepherds
rushed to the stable to worship Jesus.

*And she gave birth to her firstborn
son, and wrapped him in bands of
cloth and laid him in a manger.*

Luke 2:7

243

# The child, Jesus

244

## SIMEON AND ANNA MEET JESUS

Mary and Joseph took Jesus to the temple to give a thank-you gift to God. There, they met an old man named Simeon, who loved God. Simeon cuddled baby Jesus and whispered a prayer: "Thank you, God. Now I can die in peace."

"This baby will change the future of many people," Simeon told Mary and Joseph. They were amazed.

They were just as surprised by Anna, the old temple prophet. "Praise God!" Anna exclaimed. Anna told everyone who would listen who this baby was.

## VISITING MAGI

Wise men from the east came looking for Jesus. They made the mistake of asking King Herod for directions to the new king. Jealous Herod hatched a plot to kill him.

Jesus was toddling around the house when the wise men arrived with gifts of gold, frankincense and myrrh. Angels warned Joseph of Herod's evil plot. Fortunately, Jesus, Mary and Joseph escaped just in time.

## JESUS VISITS THE TEMPLE

When Jesus was twelve, his family went to Jerusalem to celebrate Passover. On the way home, Mary and Joseph discovered Jesus wasn't with their group. Back to Jerusalem! They found Jesus at the temple talking with the teachers, who were amazed at how much he understood. Jesus grew up and got wiser.

*Luke chapter 2 verses 22 to 52, and Matthew chapter 2 verses 1 to 15*

# The baptism of Jesus

JOHN BAPTIZES
JESUS

John preached,
"Change your ways!
Make way for God!"

"What should we
do?" people asked.

"Share what you
have. Be fair. Don't be
bullies," was John's message.

If people really had a
change of heart, John
baptized them in the Jordan
River.

John baptized Jesus. After
Jesus came out of the water,
the Spirit came down like a
dove.

A voice said, "You are my
child, my beloved."

*And the Holy Spirit
descended upon him in
bodily form, like a dove.*

Luke 3:22

# Four fishers

246

### ANDREW AND PETER

As Jesus walked along the edge of the shoreline of Lake Galilee he saw two pairs of brothers. The first two were Andrew and Peter. These young, strong, tanned fishers were busily throwing their net into the water looking for another catch of fish.

Jesus said to them, "Come and follow me. You will no longer catch fish, you will catch people. I will make you fishers for people."

At once, Andrew and Peter dropped their nets and followed Jesus.

### JAMES AND JOHN

A little further along Lake Galilee Jesus saw the second pair of brothers. James and John were in their family fishing boat with their father Zebedee.

"James and John, come and follow me," Jesus called.

At once they left their father and followed Jesus.

*As Jesus passed along the Sea of Galilee, he saw Simon and his brother Andrew casting a net into the sea — for they were fishermen.*

*Mark 1:16*

*Matthew chapter 10 verses 2 to 4, and Luke chapter 8 verses 1 to 3*

# Followers of Jesus

## FRIENDS AND APOSTLES

Jesus had many followers, friends and helpers. Some were called apostles, that is, people who were specially chosen to help Jesus in his ministry. Some famous apostles were: Simon (also called Peter), James, John, Thomas, Matthew, and Mary Magdalene. Judas was one of Jesus' apostles. How terrible it was that Judas betrayed Jesus!

## WOMEN TRAVEL WITH JESUS

Jesus went to many cities and villages telling good news about God. Twelve disciples went with him, as well as many women that Jesus had healed. These included Mary Magdalene, Joanna, Suzanna. The women used their own money to help Jesus.

### Apostles

*Apostle*
The word "apostle" means "those who are sent." Jesus chose apostles to help him in his ministry.

*Lists of 12*
Twelve was a special number — like the twelve tribes of Israel. Three gospels list twelve apostles, but the names are different. The gospel of John has no list of "twelve." Jesus probably had many special helpers.

**The twelve were with him, as well as some women who had been cured.**

*Luke 8:1-2*

# The farmer and the seed

### JESUS TELLS A STORY

A farmer planted seeds.

Some seeds fell on the path, where the birds ate it.

Some seeds fell on the rocks. The plants had no roots, so they withered in the sun.

Some seeds fell among weeds and were choked out.

But some seeds landed in good soil, where they grew well and produced a lot of grain.

### FOUR TYPES OF LISTENERS

"The farmer," explained Jesus, "is like a person who shares God's teaching.

"The four types of soil stand for four types of people who listen to God's teaching.

"The path is like people who let Satan snatch God's teaching from their minds.

"The rocky soil is like those people who are full of joy at first. But as soon as troubles come along, they collapse.

"The seeds overgrown with weeds are like people who accept God's teaching. But, later, their worries, their love of money, and their longing for everything else in life, squeezes out God's teaching.

"But the good soil is like listeners who welcome God's

teaching into their lives and follow it. They grow and grow; and share more and more love in the world."

*"Other seed fell into good soil and brought forth grain."*

Mark 4:8

*They watched him to see
whether he would cure
him on the sabbath.*

Mark 3:2

# A man with a crippled hand

As Jesus went into the synagogue he at once saw a man who had a crippled hand.

"What would Jesus do?" some people thought to themselves. "Jesus won't heal him, as it is against the law to heal anyone on the sabbath," they reckoned.

Jesus could read their minds. "Tell me, is it right to do good or to do evil on the sabbath?"

They were dumbfounded and gave no answer.

Jesus said to the crippled man, "Let me look at your hand." To everyone's great surprise, the man moved his hand and was healed.

But the Pharisees were furious. They left to hatch a plot to kill Jesus.

# Jesus heals two men

## DEMONS

There were two men who nobody wanted to meet.
They lived all by themselves in caves which were used
to bury dead people. Anybody who came near them
was attacked. Worst of all — they were full of demons.

But they came to meet Jesus. The demons in the
two men spoke to Jesus: "What do you want to do
with us, Son of God? Have you come to punish us?"

## PIGS

"If you make us leave these two men," continued the
demons, "let us go into these pigs."

Jesus commanded them with a single word: "Go!"

The demons left the men and went into the pigs.
The pigs rushed down the hill into a lake where they were
drowned.

The two men felt well and happy and smiled broadly as
they thanked Jesus for all he had done for them.

*They were so fierce that no one could pass that way.*

*Matthew 8:28*

# Jesus heals a woman

### Twelve years of illness

A certain poor woman had been ill for 12 long years. When she first felt sick, she went immediately to the doctor, but she didn't get any better. So she went to a second doctor, but still was not better. She tried every doctor in town, but no one could help her. Finally, she had no money left because she had spent all her savings on doctors' fees and medicines. Worst of all, no one wanted to go near her because of her illness.

### The woman's touch

One day the woman heard about a young man who preached and healed people. So she joined the crowd and listened

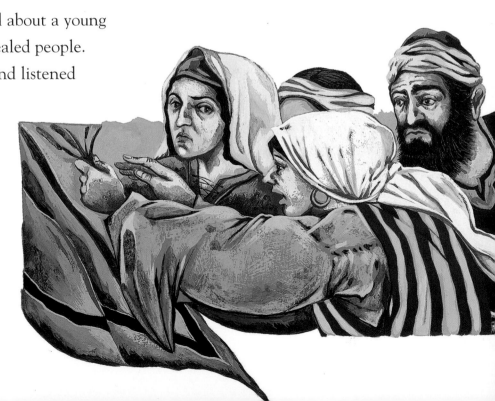

*She had heard about Jesus, and came up behind him in the crowd and touched his cloak.*

Mark 5:27

to the man, who was Jesus. Then she edged her way closer and closer to Jesus, until he was only a few feet in front of her.

Then she did it. She stretched out her hand and touched Jesus' coat. She was sure nobody would notice. But as she did this she was completely better. She knew Jesus had healed her.

## JESUS' QUESTION

As the woman touched him, Jesus felt power leave him. He stopped walking and turned round. "Who touched me?" he asked.

"Isn't that a bit of a silly question?" suggested someone. "There are so many people bumping into you all the time, how can you ask, 'Who touched me?'"

But Jesus was not put off. He continued to look around to find the person who had touched him. The woman knew that she had been discovered. Trembling, she came up to Jesus, bowed low before him, and said, "It was me." And she told Jesus why she had done it.

## A HAPPY ENDING

But she didn't need to be afraid. Jesus was not angry with her. "Dear woman," Jesus said to her gently, as he took her hand and helped her to stand upright, "you are well because you trusted in God. You will suffer no more. Go in peace."

# Jesus brings a girl back to life

254

Jairus was a very important person, the top man in his synagogue. He approached Jesus; he was desperate.

"Jesus," he said as he bowed down low, "my daughter has just died. But I know that if you touch her, she will be well."

### JESUS' TOUCH

When Jesus arrived at the dead girl's home he said, "She isn't dead, she's only sleeping." He took her hand in his hand and said, "Little girl, get up." She stood up. And everyone in her village heard about this miracle.

**Peter, James and John**
Peter, James and John were Jesus' closest friends. Jesus took them, and only them, with him at some special times.

"Jesus allowed no one to follow him except Peter, James and John" (Mark 5:37).

Jesus took these three apostles with him up a mountain where he was changed and his clothes became shining white (Mark 9:2-8).

In the Garden of Gethsemane, only Peter, James, and John were allowed to be close to Jesus, as he prayed.

*But when the crowd had been put outside, he went in and took her by the hand, and the girl got up.*

*Matthew 9:25*

# Mary and Martha

### MARTHA'S GRUMBLING

Mary and Martha might have been sisters, but they could not have been more different. They and their brother Lazarus were good friends with Jesus. They often put Jesus up for the night and gave him a meal. Their home at Bethany was just a few miles from Jerusalem.

"Won't anybody help me?" muttered Martha. "Why does Mary always sit and talk with Jesus, leaving me to do all the cooking!"

"Martha, Martha," replied Jesus soothingly, "you are fussed up about too many things. Only one thing is important. Mary has made the right choice."

*But Martha was distracted by her many tasks; so she came to him and asked, "Lord, do you not care that my sister has left me to do all the work?"*

Luke 10:40

# Everything changes

256

## GOD IS HERE

"God's time is not far off in the future," said Jesus to his close friends. They didn't get it. "God's time is right now. God's power is with us right now," Jesus explained.

A few days later, they got to see first hand what Jesus meant.

## UP THE MOUNTAIN

Jesus took his closest friends up a mountain. Before their very eyes, Jesus changed. His clothes shone as though they had been dipped in dazzling paint. Then they saw Moses and Elijah talking to Jesus.

"What should we do?" exclaimed Peter in terror. "We should make a shelter for each of them." He didn't know what he was talking about.

A cloud drifted low over the mountain and they couldn't see past the end of their noses. A voice from the cloud said, "This is my Child, the Beloved. Listen to him."

The clouds lifted, and they saw only Jesus standing there. They puzzled over what this could possibly mean.

*And from the cloud there came a voice, "This is my Son, the Beloved; listen to him."*

*Mark 9:7*

## NEW TESTAMENT
### *Chapter 16: From the Bible books of Matthew, John and Acts*

# Jesus is betrayed

INTRODUCTION

*In this chapter, we hear more about the teaching of Jesus.*

*We also read about the last meal Jesus had with his followers and the mysterious words he said about his body and blood being like bread and wine.*

*Then we read about the moment when Judas left the other followers of Jesus. He went out into the night to betray Jesus and hand him over to people who wanted Jesus killed.*

*We hear how Jesus died on the cross and came alive again three days later.*

*Then, we learn that Jesus' disciples received the Holy Spirit at the Feast of Pentecost.*

*There are a number of "firsts" in this chapter: the first recorded healing by Jesus' followers after Jesus was killed; the first Christian martyr; the first person brought back from the dead by a disciple of Jesus; and the first African to become a follower of Jesus.*

# One lost sheep

258

*"And if he finds it, truly
I tell you, he rejoices
over it more than over
the ninety-nine that
never went astray."*

Matthew 18:13

Jesus told this story about a caring shepherd who had 100 sheep.

One day one of the 100 sheep decided to go off on its own. It got lost and couldn't find its way back to the other 99 sheep. It was scared that it might be eaten by a lion, or gobbled up by a bear.

Then the sheep saw its best friend, the loving shepherd. The shepherd had left the other 99 sheep just to come looking for the lost sheep. The shepherd knew how tired and weak and hungry the lost sheep had become. He was so relieved and happy to find the little sheep that he lifted it gently onto his shoulders and carried it back to the safety of the sheepfold.

Jesus ended this story by saying: "God does not want any of God's little children to be lost."

# One lost coin

## LOOKING IN THE CORNERS

Jesus told a story about a woman who had ten silver coins but lost one.

"Now, what have I done with that tenth silver coin?" she asked herself. "I'm always putting things down and forgetting where I've put them. I don't know how I could have lost that coin."

"There's nothing for it, I'll have to look for it until I find it."

She started by lighting her oil lamp. Then she carefully swept her dusty floor. She looked in one corner of the room, then in the second corner, then in the third corner, but she found no coin. Getting desperate she swept the fourth corner. And there it was!

## "I'VE FOUND IT!"

"Wonderful," the woman shouted out. She rushed to her friends and neighbors: "Be happy with me — I've found the coin I lost."

Jesus ended this parable with the words: "In the same way, there is joy before the angels of God over one sinner who repents."

> *"Rejoice with me for I have found the coin that I had lost."*
>
> Luke 15:9

### One silver coin

The woman in Jesus' story may have lost a very precious thing. Her lost silver coin might have been equivalent to an engagement ring. If it was one of the ten silver coins which formed a headdress, it may have been part of her dowry.

The coin she lost was a drachma, a Greek coin worth a day's wages.

Looking for the coin was likely no easy matter, because her house probably had no windows. So the woman would have crawled on her hands and knees, while holding her oil lamp and feeling for the coin on her earthen floor.

259

# The "whoever's"

260

Jesus taught the people and said:

"Whoever does not take up a cross and follow me is not worthy of me."

"Whoever tries to hold on to their life will miss out on true life."

"Whoever helps one of these little ones will get their reward even if they only give a cup of cold water."

People brought children to Jesus for him to bless them. Some disciples tried to keep the children away. Jesus said, "Whoever doesn't welcome God's realm like a little child will never enter it. God's reign belongs to children." Then Jesus blessed them.

*"Whoever gives even a cup of cold water to one of these little ones in the name of a disciple — truly I tell you, none of these will lose their reward."*

*Matthew 10:42*

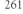

*John chapter 15 verses 1 to 9, and Matthew chapter 6 verses 8 to 13*

# Jesus is like a vine

### "I AM THE TRUE VINE"

Jesus said to the disciples:

"I am the vine; God is the gardener. God cuts off branches that don't produce fruit and trims branches that produce fruit. I am the vine, and you are the branches. Those with me produce much fruit."

### A SPECIAL PRAYER

Jesus said, "Pray like this:

our Father, Holy One,

May your time come, may your will be done in earth as in heaven.

Give us the bread we need for today.

Forgive our debts as we have forgiven the debts of others.

Keep us safe always."

*I am the vine, you are the branches.*
*Those who abide in me and I in them*
*bear much fruit.*

John 15:5

**Vines**

In the Hebrew Scriptures, vines, which bear juicy grapes for eating and for wine-making, represent God's people Israel. They were thought of as being God's vine. A bunch of grapes was carved on the outside of most synagogues. Vineyards, surrounded by walls and with a watchtower to keep a look-out for enemies, came to symbolize the land of Judah.

*Jesus the true vine*

The writers of John's gospel were Jews who were familiar with this imagery. They called Jesus "the true vine."

261

# The special meal

### PASSOVER

It was Passover, the festival when Jews remember how God freed the Israelites from slavery in Egypt. On Thursday evening, Jesus planned a Passover meal with his friends.

### BREAD

At the meal, Jesus did something his friends remembered after he was dead. It helped them to understand what happened later.

While they were eating supper, Jesus took some bread. He thanked God for it and broke it. Then he gave it to his followers. He said, "Take this bread and eat. This bread is my body."

### WINE

After the meal, Jesus took a goblet of wine, thanked God and gave it to the followers. Jesus said, "Drink this. This is my blood, which is poured out for many, to forgive sins."

### ONE MORE CLUE

Jesus gave his followers one more clue by talking about heaven. He said, "I will not drink any more wine until I drink it new with you in God's realm."

# Judas the betrayer

### JESUS' SOLEMN ANNOUNCEMENT

Jesus was eating the last meal he would have with his disciples. "One of you is going to turn against me," Jesus said sadly.

His friends looked at each other with dismay. "Who's he talking about?" they whispered to each other.

The disciple whom Jesus specially loved was sitting next to Jesus. So Peter nodded to him and said, "Ask Jesus who he is talking about."

The disciple leaned over to Jesus and asked, "Who is going to betray you, Lord?"

Jesus said, "The person I give this bread to is the one." Jesus then took a piece of bread, dipped it in a dish, and gave it to Judas.

### JUDAS GOES INTO THE NIGHT

Judas took the bread. Immediately, Judas left the table and went out. It was night.

*So, after receiving the bread, he [Judas] immediately went out. And it was night.*

*John 13:30*

# Jesus dies, but comes back to life

264

### THE SOLDIERS

The soldiers arrested Jesus. Jesus was put on trial and whipped. The Roman soldiers nailed Jesus to the cross. Some of Jesus' friends, including Peter, ran away in fear, but Mary Magdalene and the other women stayed.

### JESUS LOVES TO THE END

Jesus saw his mother, Mary, and John, at the foot of his cross.

Jesus said to Mary, "Here is your son." To John, Jesus said, "Here is your mother." So John took Mary to live in his home.

### JESUS DIES

A little later, Jesus said in a clear, loud voice, "It is finished." He bowed his head and died.

*John chapters 19 and 20*

**Mary Magdalene came to the tomb and saw that the stone had been removed from the tomb.**

*John 19:30; 20:1*

### JESUS IS BURIED

A man named Joseph, from Arimathea, and a leading rabbi named Nicodemus took the body of Jesus, wrapped it and laid it in a tomb. This was the usual way Jews buried their dead.

### JESUS' TOMB IS EMPTY

Just before dawn Mary Magdalene went to Jesus' tomb. Mary saw that the large stone had been mysteriously rolled away. She looked in the tomb. Jesus' body was gone! As Mary stood crying she heard a voice say, "Mary." It was Jesus! Mary rushed off to tell the others, "I have seen Jesus!"

265

*Acts chapter 2 verses 1 to 13*

# The Holy Spirit comes

*All of them were filled with the Holy Spirit.*

*Acts 2:4*

### WAITING

Jesus' disciples had seen the risen Lord Jesus many times after he had come alive. For forty days they listened to his every word. "Don't leave Jerusalem," he told them. "Wait here until you receive the Holy Spirit."

### WIND, FIRE, AND DIFFERENT LANGUAGES

So the disciples waited. Then, on the day of Pentecost, it happened.

They heard a strange noise: like a mighty wind blowing.

They saw flames of fire — one flame of fire on top of each person.

They spoke in a variety of languages.

### POWER FROM GOD

The Holy Spirit had arrived to give Jesus' followers power from God. In the strength of this power they preached and healed people.

# Peter heals a man

### THE BEAUTIFUL GATE

It was nearly three o'clock. Peter and John were on their way to pray at the temple. As they came to the temple gate called Beautiful Gate, they saw a man sitting on the ground — he had never been able to walk.

### "STAND UP AND WALK!"

Peter stretched out his hand and took hold of the man's right hand and helped him stand up. At once the man's ankles and feet were made strong. He went into the temple, jumping for joy and giving thanks to God for this wonderful miracle.

*When he saw Peter and John about to go into the temple, he asked them for alms.*

Acts 3:3

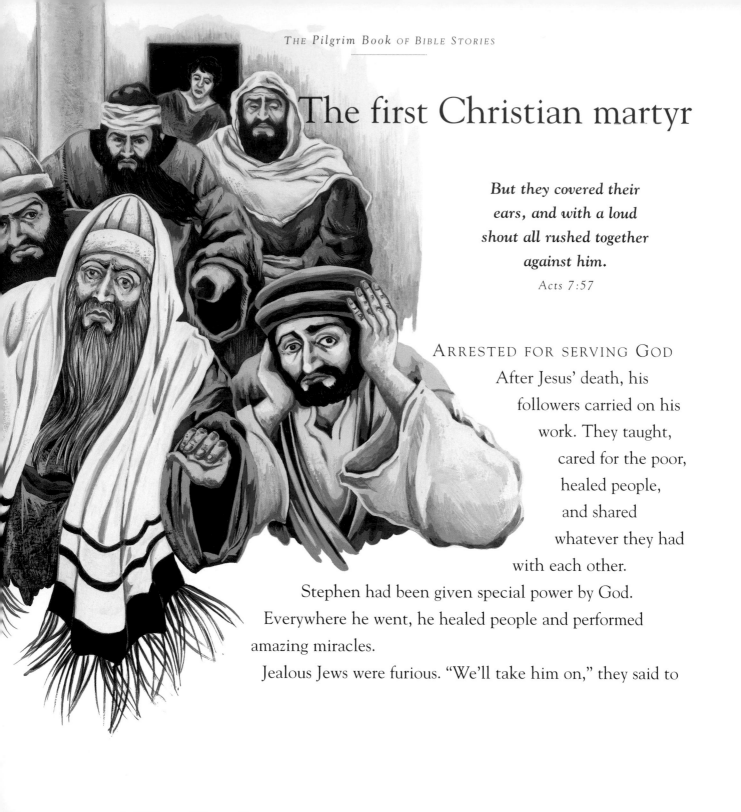

# The first Christian martyr

*But they covered their
ears, and with a loud
shout all rushed together
against him.*

Acts 7:57

### ARRESTED FOR SERVING GOD

After Jesus' death, his
followers carried on his
work. They taught,
cared for the poor,
healed people,
and shared
whatever they had
with each other.

Stephen had been given special power by God.
Everywhere he went, he healed people and performed
amazing miracles.

Jealous Jews were furious. "We'll take him on," they said to each other. And they argued against him. But the more they argued, the more everyone else saw how wise Stephen was.

That was the last straw. They grabbed Stephen and brought him before the Jewish leaders. "We charge the accused with saying that Jesus will change the things Moses has taught us. He even said that Jesus of Nazareth will destroy the temple."

All eyes were on Stephen. As he began his defense, everyone saw that his face was like that of an angel.

## STEPHEN'S DEFENSE

Stephen started to accuse his accusers. "How stubborn you are!" said Stephen. "You've set your hearts against God. You won't listen to the Holy Spirit."

## STEPHEN IS KILLED

The Jewish leaders had had enough. They ground their teeth in anger. They went for Stephen, dragged him outside the walls of Jerusalem, and threw rocks and large stones at him. Stephen did not try to defend himself, but just prayed, "Jesus, receive my spirit!" One stone hit Stephen on the forehead and he fell to his knees. Stephen summoned up all his remaining strength for a last prayer, "Lord, do not hold this sin against them!"

# Philip and the Ethiopian

270

### AN ETHIOPIAN OFFICIAL

Philip had a vision of angels urging him to go to a road in the wilderness.

There he saw a magnificent chariot. It belonged to an Ethiopian, a high official in the queen's court. In fact, this man was so important he was in charge of all the queen's money. The Ethiopian had come to Jerusalem to worship and was returning home.

### PHILIP TALKS ABOUT JESUS

Philip went over to the chariot and walked along beside it. The Ethiopian was reading the scroll of the prophet Isaiah. "Do you understand it?" Philip asked.

"How can I?" replied the Ethiopian. "I don't have anyone to teach me."

Philip explained that the prophet Isaiah was talking about a person God would send to save God's people. Then Philip told the Ethiopian all about Jesus.

### A NEW FOLLOWER

The Ethiopian believed instantly. "I want to become a follower of Jesus," he declared. He commanded the chariot to stop and Philip baptized him right on the spot.

# Peter and Dorcas

The followers of Jesus performed many miracles after they received the Holy Spirit. They were very upset when one of them, a lady called Dorcas, died.

Peter went to the upstairs room where she lay.

When he managed to empty the room of all the sad people he kneeled and prayed. Then he turned toward Dorcas' body and said, "Dorcas, stand up!" Her eyes opened. Peter held out his hand, and helped her to her feet.

*All the widows stood beside him, weeping and showing tunics and other clothing that Dorcas had made while she was with them.*

Acts 9:39

# Living for God

272

## LIVE IN PEACE

Jesus' followers continued to spread the good news and heal people. They impressed everyone around them with the love and care they showed. Paul summed up their attitude in advice he gave to followers in Rome.

"Bless those who persecute you; bless and do not curse them.

Rejoice with those who rejoice, weep with those who weep.

Live in harmony with one another;

do not be haughty, but associate with the lowly;

do not claim to be wiser than you are.

Do not repay anyone evil for evil,

but take thought for what is noble in the sight of all.

If it is possible, so far as it depends on you,

live peaceably with all." (NRSV)

*Rejoice with those who rejoice, weep with those who weep.*

Romans 12:15

NEW TESTAMENT

*Chapter 17: From the Bible books of Romans, 1 Corinthians, 2 Corinthians, Galatians, Ephesians, Philippians, Colossians and Thessalonians*

# Paul's tough letters

INTRODUCTION

*This chapter guides us through some of the letters Paul and his followers wrote to different groups of Christians.*

*The style in the letters seems sometimes quite sharp and stern. Paul wanted to bring people to their senses, or bring them back to the beliefs and ways of living that he had taught them. In these following pages we read of Paul calling the Christians at Corinth "babies," and telling them off for boasting.*

*Paul gives plenty of positive advice as well. Writing to the Christians at Galatia he lists the things that they should not do and then lists nine qualities they should have in their lives.*

*In his letter to the Ephesians Paul tells them the sort of things they should not say, and then the sort of things they should say.*

*Paul gives great words of encouragement in his first letter to the Thessalonians, as they face their troubles without him.*

# A right telling off

274

WHO IS PAUL?

Paul never met Jesus in person. In fact, Paul had once hated the Christians and everything they did. He spied on them, hunted them down, and even handed them over to the Romans to be put in prison or killed.

Then, one day Paul had an amazing vision. He saw a blinding light, and in a flash, Paul heard Jesus speaking directly to him. Paul became a believer who was willing to risk his own life for Jesus. He traveled all over the Roman empire sharing the good news about Jesus Christ.

Some of Jesus' followers had a lot to learn. The apostle Paul, who had been a top rabbi, was an excellent teacher.

*And so, brothers and sisters, I could not speak to you as spiritual people but . . . as infants in Christ.*

*1 Corinthians 3:1*

# "How you boast!"

## CHRISTIANS AT CORINTH

Writing to new followers of Jesus in the town of Corinth, Paul had a lot of wrongs to put right.

"You're living like all the wicked people around you," Paul challenged them. "When I visited you," Paul continued, "I had to treat you like little babies. And even now, you are behaving like babies, not like the age you are.

"How you love to boast," Paul continued. "You act as if you were strong and rich but you are really feeble and poor when it comes to trusting God. While you go around saying how strong you are, we are weak."

"Look at us," said Paul. "People curse us, but we bless them. They hurt us, and we accept it."

*We are hungry and thirsty, we are poorly clothed and beaten and homeless.*

1 Corinthians 4:11

# New ways to live

276

### A LITTLE NEW YEAST

"Your boasting will get you nowhere," warned Paul.

"You know that just one spoonful of new yeast mixed into a big bowl of dough causes the dough to rise and become good loaves of bread."

"You've got to get rid of the old yeast in your lives. Then you will be like a new batch of dough."

"Remember," continued Paul, "Jesus is the one who died to make us good and to make us pure."

### LOVE IS . . .

Even if I could speak like an angel, if I didn't have love I'd be like a clanging gong. I could be a genius, a superhero, or even a saint, but if I didn't have love, what good would that be?

Love is patient and kind. Love is not envious. It doesn't boast or insist on its own way. Love is not

**1 Corinthians chapter 5 verses 6 to 8, chapter 13, and 2 Corinthians chapter 9 verses 1 to 15**

*It is written: "He scatters abroad; he gives to the poor; his righteousness endures forever."*

*2 Corinthians 9:9*

irritable or resentful. It doesn't laugh at bad news, but is happy when people are truthful. Love puts up with anything. Love believes. And love hopes.

Fine speeches come to an end, but love never ends.

## Be generous

"You Corinthians must give generously," stated Paul, "especially since I've told our fellow-Christians in Macedonia about your generosity. "And make sure that, whatever you give, you give with joy."

*Then after three years I did go up to Jerusalem to meet with Cephas [Peter] and stayed with him fifteen days.*

Galatians 1:18

# Paul's tough letter

### "LISTEN TO ME"

"You've got to listen to my teaching, you Christians of Galatia," insisted Paul. "It's not that I'm boasting, it's because God has given me a message that you must accept. You see my sermons and letters are not full of my own thoughts and ideas. Rather, they are God's wisdom that has been given to me."

## My message is from God

"After my moment of hearing Jesus speak to me on the road to Damascus, I didn't rush off to Jerusalem and learn from the other disciples. No. I was taught directly by God. So what I now say comes from God."

*For I want you to know, brothers and sisters, that the gospel that was proclaimed by me is not of human origin.*

*Galatians 1:11*

279

## Peter gets it wrong

"Even Peter gave in to those who wanted new believers to obey the old Jewish laws," Paul continued. "As soon as Jews came on the scene Peter would no longer eat with non-Jewish people. I spoke to him face to face: 'Peter, you are a Jew, but you are not living like a Jew. So why do you try to force non-Jews to live like Jews?' You must see it, you Galatians; the only thing that matters is our faith in Jesus."

280

## Lists about how to live

Paul give three other lists in his letters about how Jesus' followers are meant to live.

*2 Corinthians*
In his second letter to the Christians at Corinth Paul says, "We show we are servants of God by living a pure life, by our understanding, by our patience, and by our kindness. . . . by true love, by speaking the truth . . ." (2 Corinthians 6:6, 7).

*Ephesians*
"Always be humble and gentle. Be patient and accept each other with love" (Ephesians 4:2).

*Colossians*
"Show mercy to others; be kind, humble, gentle, and patient. Do not be angry with each other, but forgive each other. If someone does wrong to you, then forgive him" (Colossians 3:12, 13).

# Two ways

"Let me tell you about two ways of living, fellow-Christians who live in Galatia," wrote Paul.

### THE WRONG WAY

"Here's a list of things which are clearly sinful: impure thoughts and actions, worshiping idols, witchcraft, hating people, causing trouble, being jealous, losing your temper, envying other people, being drunk, going on binges.

"I've warned you before that people who do these things don't belong to God's kingdom."

281

## THE RIGHT WAY

"The right way to live, as a follower of Jesus," continued Paul, "is to live under the control of God and the Spirit. The Spirit gives love, joy, peace, patience, kindness, goodness, faithfulness, gentleness, self-control.

"Our new life comes from the Spirit, so we pay attention to the Spirit and are guided by the Spirit."

*If we live by the Spirit,*
*let us also be guided*
*by the Spirit.*

Galations 5:25

# Paul writes to the Ephesians

282

*Put away from you all bitterness and wrath and anger and wrangling.*

Ephesians 4:31

### WHEN YOU TALK

"This is how you should speak," wrote Paul to the Ephesians. "Do not say hurtful things. Use helpful words that make people feel better and stronger."

"Do not be nasty to people. Do not yell at them or make them feel stupid."

### FORGIVE

"Never do wrong things," Paul went on to write. "Be kind and loving."

"Forgive one another just as God forgave you in Christ."

### TAKE CARE HOW YOU LIVE

"Watch how you live," warned Paul.

"Do not live like fools. Be wise.

"Do good whenever you have the chance, because these are bad times.

"Be filled with the Spirit, not drunk with wine."

## SAYING THANKS TO GOD

"When you are with your Christian friends, sing psalms and hymns and spiritual songs.

"Sing in your hearts to God, always thanking him for everything."

*Be filled with the Spirit, as you sing psalms and hymns and spiritual songs among yourselves.*

Ephesians 5:18-19

284

# Advice to the Christians at Philippi

## Keep going

"This is what you, my dear friends who live in Philippi, should do," wrote Paul.

"Keep on working out your salvation. Do this with fear and trembling, because you are in God's presence. And remember that God is with you and works in you to help you obey him. He gives you the desire and the ability to do what you should."

## Be a star

"Do everything without grumbling or arguing," continued Paul.

"Look around you. You live in a wicked world with wicked people doing evil things. You must shine like stars in this world."

*. . . so that you may be blameless and innocent, children of God.*

Philippians 2:15

*Philippians chapter 2 verses 12 to 16, and Colossians chapter 1 verses 10 to 14*

**Paul's letters**

There are 13 letters in the Bible that bear the name of the apostle Paul. Some he wrote. Others were written after his death, in his name.

There are nine letters to groups of Christians who lived in one area or city: Galatians, First Thessalonians, Second Thessalonians, First Corinthians, Second Corinthians, Romans, Colossians, Ephesians and Philippians.

There are four letters to individuals: Philemon, First Timothy, Second Timothy and Titus

285

*. . . so that you may lead lives worthy of the Lord, fully pleasing to him, as you bear fruit in every good work and as you grow in the knowledge of God.*

Colossians 1:10

# Paul's letter to the Colossians

## BE FRUITFUL

"My dear fellow-believers who live in Colosse, this is how you must live:

"You've got to live the kind of life that pleases Jesus and brings him honor.

"You've got to be like trees from which people pick lots and lots of fresh, juicy fruit. The kind of fruit I'm talking about is doing good and growing in your understanding of God."

## GOD'S POWER

"You'll be able to do all this," said Paul, "only if you rely on God and God's great power. God will make you so strong inside that you will be able to do all this."

# Paul's first letter to the Christians at Thessalonica

286

*Paul, Silvanus, and Timothy. To the church of the Thessalonians . . . Grace to you, and peace.*

1 Thessalonians 1:1

## TROUBLES

Paul wrote lots and lots of letters. Paul founded a church in the city of Thessalonica. All the members were new followers of Jesus. He had to leave them suddenly, so he dashed off this letter to help them.

## PERSECUTION

Paul knew that these new Christians would face many troubles and difficulties, so he wrote to encourage them in their faith in Jesus.

"We sent Timothy to strengthen and encourage you in your faith so that none of you would be put off

### Letter writing

*Who is the letters from?*
If we don't recognize the postmark, or the handwriting, or the address at the top of the letter, the first thing we do when we open a letter is to see who it is from. We have to go right to the end of the letter to find this out. But in Paul's day, they told you who the letter was from at the start of the letter. So Paul starts his letter, "From Paul, Silas, and Timothy" (1 Thessalonians 1:1).

*Who is the letter to?*
Next, the letter says who it is addressed to: "To the church in Thessalonica . . ."

In Paul's day, letters gave a greeting. Paul wrote a Christian form of greeting to the Thessalonians: "May God's grace and peace be yours."

287

by these attacks on our
faith. They are part of
God's plan for us. We
warned you to be ready
for trouble, but when I
heard that you were
under attack I very
much wanted to know
if you were standing
firm. This is why I sent
Timothy to you."

*Aspire to live quietly,
to mind your own
affairs, and to work
with your hands, as we
directed you.*

1 Thessalonians 4:11

*1 Thessalonians chapter 5 verses 1 to 11*

# Jesus will return

### BE READY

The first Christians believed that Jesus would come back to be with them very soon. When that didn't happen they got discouraged. But Paul assured them, "The day will come when we least expect it. The day will come like a thief does, in the middle of the night, when we are least expecting it.

### BE ARMED

"So keep alert. Be prepared for Jesus' return," continued Paul.

"We're in a battle against evil. In battles, warriors wear clothes to protect themselves. In this battle, you don't need armor, you need faith and love to protect you. And on your head you should put the helmet called 'the hope of salvation.'"

*For you yourselves know very well that the day of the Lord will come like a thief in the night.*

*1 Thessalonians 5:2*

# New Testament

## Chapter 18: From the Bible books of 2 Thessalonians, 1 Timothy, 2 Timothy, Titus, Philemon and James

# Paul's tender letters

### Introduction

*Some Christians at Thessalonica stopped working because they thought Jesus was about to return. A letter from Paul sets them straight — "Keep doing what is right."*

*In Paul's two letters to Timothy we see how fond the writer was of Timothy. And the young Timothy gets lots of advice on the importance of prayer, on what to look for in a good church leader, on the lure of money, and on the value of the Scriptures. Also included in this book are some of the last words ever written by Paul.*

*The letter to Titus contains more friendly advice from Paul, while a letter from Paul to Philemon makes a request for a loving welcome on behalf of a runaway slave.*

*This book ends with down-to-earth teaching from James — about caring for poor people and controlling your anger.*

*"Now we command you, beloved, in the name of our Lord Jesus Christ, to keep away from believers who are living in idleness and not according to the tradition that they received from us."*

2 Thessalonians 3:6

# "Keep working"

Some of the Christians at Thessalonica stopped working. "If Jesus is coming back so soon, why bother?" they thought. "We can all just go home and wait for the end of the world to happen."

They had the wrong idea. Someone wrote them a letter to get this sorted out. The letter was probably from one of Paul's followers, but the letter is written in Paul's name to make sure the believers pay attention.

## KEEP CLEAR

"People who refuse to work aren't following the teaching that Paul gave," the letter explained. "Sisters and brothers, you shouldn't even hang around with other believers who are acting this way."

## PAUL'S EXAMPLE

Paul was a tentmaker. He was skillful at stitching together the heavy canvas. When Paul visited Christians in other cities, he took his work with him. This way, he earned money to help pay for his room and board.

"Don't forget the example that we gave you," the letter continues. "You should live as we live. We were not lazy when we visited you. When we ate someone else's food, we always paid for it."

## MY OWN HAND

The letter ends with the curious note: "See I am writing with my own hand." This suggests that whoever wrote the letter had poor handwriting and used a scribe to put most of the words on parchment. Then they added a note in their own handwriting just to prove it was from them.

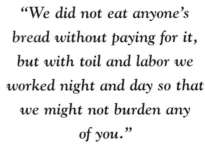

*"We did not eat anyone's*
*bread without paying for it,*
*but with toil and labor we*
*worked night and day so that*
*we might not burden any*
*of you."*

*2 Thessalonians 3:8*

# Letters to Timothy

292

### A GROWING CHURCH

The little groups of Christians grew bigger. They chose church leaders, and bishops. But, just as Paul had done, they still wrote letters to each other.

Years after Paul died, someone sent a letter. "Imagine that I'm Paul, said the writer, "and you are his beloved friend, Timothy. Imagine what Paul would say if he were still alive."

### MY CHILD

"Timothy, you are like my own special child. Don't be timid. Be a good leader in the church. Do all the things that we know you can do. It is as though we're in a military battle. We're in a struggle about faith, and we have to keep a firm grip on what we believe."

*I am giving you these instructions, Timothy my child . . . so that by following them you may fight the good fight having faith.*

1 Timothy 1:18

293

*I desire, then, that in
every place the men
should pray, lifting up
holy hands without anger
or argument.*

1 Timothy 2:8

### Letters to Timothy

Timothy, a friend and
helper who traveled with
the Paul, later became an
important church leader.
The two letters aren't
actually from Paul himself,
they are composed as if Paul
were writing to Timothy.

The language is different
from Paul's, especially in the
original Greek. Also, the
church has changed a lot.
The letter mentions things
that didn't exist in Paul's
day, such as bishops, elders
and deacons.

Paul worked with many
strong women who were
leaders in the early church.
This letter says only men
should speak in church and
women should be silent,
contradicting the way Paul
treated women.

## PRAYER

Now, Timothy, I want to tell you about praying to
God:

Pray for everyone, because God doesn't leave
anyone out. God wants everyone to know the truth.

Don't hold up angry fists. Instead, hold your
hands up in prayer.

Don't dress up in fancy clothes when
you go to pray. It's far more
important to do things that
please God. Help other
people, especially the
poor.

# More advice for the church

*Let them manage their
children and their
households well.*

1 Timothy 3:12

WHAT MAKES A GOOD
CHURCH LEADER?
By the time of this letter,
the church had many
different leaders —church
members, bishops,
deacons, and elders.
Today, the work these
leaders do may be
different, but the kind of
person they must be
remains the same.

This letter describes
what makes a good leader:

"Good church leaders
are gentle, wise, and calm.
They aren't violent or
aggressive.

**1 Timothy chapter 3 verses 1 to 13, and chapter 6 verses 6 to 10**

*For the love of money is a root of all kinds of evil,
and in their eagerness to be rich some have
wandered away from the faith.*

1 Timothy 6:10

"They care well for their own families. If they can't do that, how can they possibly care for the church family?

"Good leaders are people that others trust and respect. They welcome other people into their homes. They're not conceited. They take what they do seriously. They don't lie or put other people down. They aren't greedy for money."

## MONEY MATTERS

"Let's get it straight about money. If we have our basic needs, like enough food to eat and clothes to wear, we should be contented people.

"People who long to become rich fall into a trap. People who want to be rich are swamped by temptation. They run after lots of foolish things, which only gives them trouble. Wanting to have lots and lots of money has made some people stop following Jesus. In the end, having a great love for money only brings sadness."

# Timid Timothy

### TIMOTHY'S FAITH

The writer of the second letter to Timothy imagines what Paul would say if he was writing to his young friend:

"Timothy, I miss you very much, just as you miss me. How I recall our tearful goodbye. I long to see you again. That would make me full of joy.

"I remember you all the time in my prayers, both night and day.

"I know that your faith is strong. This is the same

*I am reminded of your sincere faith, a faith that lived first in your grandmother Lois, your mother Eunice and now, I am sure, in you.*

2 Timothy 1:5

READ-THE-STORY-FOR-YOURSELF
....................................
*2 Timothy chapter 1 verses 1 to 7, and chapter 2 verses 20 to 26*

297

faith that your mother, Eunice, and your grandmother Lois, had. Timothy, remember to use the gift that God gave you when I laid my hands on your head. This special gift from God must grow. It must be like a tiny flame that is fanned into a raging fire.

"Don't be a timid Timothy. The spirit God has given us makes us brave. God's Spirit fills us with power and love and self-control."

## A WORKER FOR GOD

"Now, Timothy, I know that you long to work for God. As God's worker, do not be ashamed to speak out for the Lord Jesus, and do not be ashamed because I am a prisoner.

"A house is full of special things made of gold and silver. But it also has many things made of wood and clay. Think of yourself as one of those special things, to be used for something important."

*In a large house there are utensils . . . some for special use, some for ordinary.*

2 Timothy 2:20

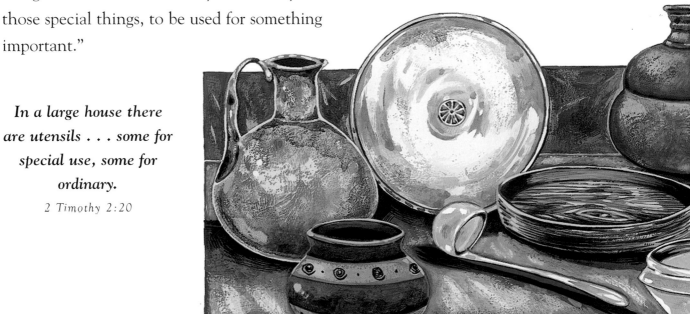

# The Scriptures

298

WISDOM

The second letter to
Timothy gave good
advice to the Christians:

"Continue to follow what you have
learned, and remember what you have been
taught. You know that you can trust your
teachers."

The Christians who received this letter were Jews.
Ever since they were little children, they had heard the
Hebrew scriptures — the words of the prophets, the psalms, the
stories of Noah, Abraham, Sarah, Hagar, Joseph, Moses, Miriam,
and all the others. This is what the writer had to say about the sacred
Jewish writing:

"All these sacred texts, given by God, teach us how to live. God has
breathed wisdom into the words. They make us wise enough to put our
trust in Jesus, who makes us whole."

*From childhood you have known the sacred*
*writings that are able to instruct you.*

*2 Timothy 3:15*

**2 Timothy chapter 3 verses 14 to 17, and chapter 4 verses 9 to 18**

# Final words

299

The writer of this letter had some final, personal words: "I am almost all alone here in prison. When I first went on trial, no one helped me. In fact, everyone deserted me. I beg you, come and see me just as soon as you can.

"And when you come, bring my friend Mark along with you. He's a very useful person to have around. It's freezing here in prison, so please bring my coat with you, the one I left with Carpus. At least that will stop me from dying of cold.

"And when you come, bring those scrolls of mine — the ones which have scriptures written on them. I can't bear being separated from them. Reading them makes me feel better.

"I'm about to leave this world, my dear friend. May the Lord bring me safely to his kingdom in heaven. Goodbye and may the Lord be with you."

*When you come, bring the cloak I left with Carpus at Troas, also the books, and above all the parchments.*

2 Timothy 4:13

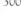
# A letter to Titus

300

## WHO IS TITUS?

Titus was another of Paul's friends and helpers. Titus often traveled with Paul as he went from city to city telling people about Jesus. Titus delivered one of Paul's letter to Christians in the city of Corinth.

One of the letters in our Bible is written to Titus. It is another example of someone writing in Paul's name, after Paul had died.

## ADVICE

"Titus, you are like a true son to me. Here is some advice to help you and others in the church:

"Older people can help young men and women learn about God's ways. They should be good role models, doing what is good. They should be strong in faith, strong in love, and strong in patience.

"Remember that God loves us just because God is kind, not because of what we do. We don't earn God's love: it's a free gift."

**For the grace of God has appeared, bringing salvation to all.**

*Titus 2:11*

# Philemon

Paul wrote this letter to a man named Philemon. The person who delivered the letter for Paul was a runaway slave named Onesimus.

My dear friend Philemon,

Whenever I pray for you, I always thank God. I keep hearing how loving you are. It's love like yours that keeps me going here in prison.

Onesimus ran away from you. He has been helping me in prison. He has become like a son to me, and I wish he could stay. I am sending him back to you, but he is no longer to be your slave; he is your brother.

So, welcome him as you would welcome me. And while I think of it, can you get your guest room ready for me too. As soon as I get out of prison, I want to visit you.

Love, Paul

# Teaching from James

302

## LOOKING INTO A MIRROR

People who hear God's word but don't do anything are like those who look at themselves in a mirror and instantly forget what they look like. They may have

messy hair or jam on their nose. Their reflection looks terrible, but they look away and do nothing about it. What good is that? It's the same with faith. Faith without loving action is useless. You must be doers of the word, not just hearers.

*For if a person with gold
rings and in fine clothes
comes into your assembly,
and if a poor person in dirty
clothes also comes in . . .*

James 2:2

303

## RICH PERSON, POOR PERSON

"You must never think that one person is more
important than another person," James continued in
his letter.

"Suppose two very different people arrive in your
church. The first one is dressed smartly in designer
clothes, with gold rings, gold bracelets and a silver watch. At the same time another
person arrives, with no jewelry, no watch. In place of fine clothes, the poor person
wears a threadbare overcoat, torn jeans, and shoes full of holes.

"You rush up to the first one and say: 'Good morning, we're so pleased to see you.
Would you like to sit here in the best seat in the church?' But you practically ignore
the one in shabby clothes. 'I suppose you can come in. Just stand over there in the
corner where nobody will notice you.' Do not act like that."

# Watch your tongue

304

"Your tongue may be one of the smallest parts of your body, but it is one of the most powerful," warned James in his letter.

"If you can control your tongue, you've managed to bring all of yourself under control. It's like a sailing ship set at full sail in a strong wind. Just the slightest push on the rudder and the whole boat changes course, even though the rudder is so tiny.

"Or, think of a fire. From one little match a whole forest can be set ablaze. It's just like that with the tongue. It has the power to change a person's life, for better or worse. So tame your tongue. Use it to help people and to praise God."

*How great a forest is set ablaze by a small fire. And the tongue is a fire!*

James 3:5-6

# Secrets from the book of Revelation

INTRODUCTION

*This chapter dips into some of the shortest of the letters in the New Testament as well as into its most mysterious book, the book of Revelation.*

*The writer of Peter offers mature wisdom about how to serve God.*

*The writer of John speaks about light and love.*

*The writer of Revelation was a prisoner on the island of Patmos because of his faith. He wrote words of encouragement, comfort and hope to Christians who were also facing persecution. But he wrote in a kind of code. He wrote to seven churches in Asia, encouraging them and also challenging them. And he shared a vision of hope, a time when troubles would end.*

# Adding to your faith

**2 Peter**

The leader of Jesus' 12 apostles was Peter the fisher. He was quick to speak, and after Jesus was killed, Peter became the leading Christian preacher. Peter was martyred in Rome in 64 or 65 C.E. The second letter of Peter was written around 80 to 90 C.E. It isn't really a letter and it wasn't written by Peter. It's a sermon in the form of a letter. The writer followed the tradition of attributing authorship to a great past leader. By writing in Peter's name, the author was able to present Peter's teaching and defend it to opponents.

"What are the things that, when added to each other, equal a strong follower of Jesus?" asked Peter at the start of his second letter.

"I'll tell you: You start with having faith in Jesus.

To this faith, add goodness.

To your goodness, add knowledge.

To your knowledge, add self-control.

To your self-control, add the ability to keep going.

To your ability to keep going, add devotion to God.

To your devotion to God, add kindness to other followers of Jesus.

To your kindness to other followers of Jesus, add love.

"Once all these things are part of you, you will know more about Jesus, and your life will be a better and better one. And don't forget this. It was God who chose you to be followers in the first place. So keep working at showing to everyone else who you belong to."

"If you remember these things you won't fail. If you act on them you will be part of the kingdom that Jesus promises. I'll do my best to keep reminding you. You must never forget these things."

*For this very reason, you must make every effort to support your faith with goodness.*

*2 Peter 1:5*

# Walking in the light

308

### GOD IS LIGHT

"This is the message we had from God. Now we are passing it on to you," wrote John at the start of his first letter. "God is light. There is no hint of darkness about God.

"This means that if we say we are God's friends yet often do bad things, then we are plain stupid, plain liars, plain lying through our teeth. While we pretend to be walking in the light, we are really stumbling along in the dark."

*This is the message we have heard from Jesus and proclaim to you, that God is light.*

1 John 1:5

*Whoever loves a brother
or sister lives in the
light, and in such a
person there is no cause
for stumbling.*

1 John 2:10

## HOW TO LIVE IN THE LIGHT

"Someone might say, 'I live in the light, I'm a really good person.' But let me tell you — if you hate others, you are walking in the dead of night. If you hate friends, other followers of Jesus, or everyone in sight, you don't have any idea what it's like to walk in the light. You're lost in total darkness. You trip and stumble and hurt yourself because you can't see where you are going. You're like a child, wearing a blindfold and bumping into all the furniture."

# Good and evil

## LOVE EACH OTHER

"I'm not writing anything new to you. You've had this teaching from the time you first followed Jesus. In a nutshell, we must love each other," continued John in his first letter.

## CAIN AND ABEL

"Do you remember that story in the sacred Hebrew Scriptures about Cain and Abel? Cain did many evil things. Cain hated his brother so much that he killed him. Why did he do this? Because Abel did good things. You must in no way be like Cain, who lived in the grip of the Evil One."

*God is love, and those who abide in love abide in God, and God abides in them.*

1 John 4:16

**1 John chapter 3 verses 11 to 18 and chapter 5 verses 1 to 5**

311

## YOU WILL BE HATED

"So don't be surprised if there are still people in the world today like Cain. You may very well find yourself hated just because you do good. But we know that we have left the realm of death and have crossed over the bridge into the realm of life. We know this because of our love for other followers of Jesus.

"If you don't love, then you still live in the land of darkness. And if you hate your brother or sister, then you are no better than Cain. But we show that we are loving people by the good that we do."

## HOW TO BE A CONQUEROR

In the last chapter of John's first letter, chapter 5, verse 5, he writes: "Who is it that conquers the world but the one who believes that Jesus is the Son of God?" (NRSV)

*I am writing to you, young people, because you are strong and the word of God abides in you.*

1 John 2:14

# The church in Ephesus

312

## The book of Revelation

*A time of persecution*
Revelation, the last book in the Bible, is mysterious and hard to understand. It was written in a time of terrible persecution. Christians were being put in prison or killed. The writer, a man named John, was a prisoner himself. He wanted to give hope and comfort, so people wouldn't give up.

John used many strange symbols, objects, and pictures. Sometimes he used a code. If people who hated Christians read it, they wouldn't understand it. We need to de-code it when we read it today.

*The code*
The name of the book "Revelation" means to uncover something. It discloses things about God.

*Numbers*
Numbers are symbolic. The number 7, for example, stands for perfection or completion. In this book you will find seven churches, seven angels, seven golden lampstands, seven trumpets, and seven crowns, among many other sevens.

*Names of Jesus*
This book has many different names for Jesus.

He is called: the faithful witness (1:5); the ruler of the kings of the earth (1:5); the Alpha [first] and the Omega [last] (1:8); the Lion (5:5); the Lamb (5:6); Lord of lords (17:14); King of kings (17:14).

SEVEN CHURCHES
This is the message of Jesus Christ to the seven churches in Asia: Ephesus, Smyrna, Pergamum, Thyatira, Sardis, Philadelphia, and Laodicea:

"The first message is for the church of Ephesus:

"The One speaking to you [that is, the Lord Jesus Christ] walks among the seven golden lampstands [that is, the churches of Asia]. In my right hand of power and authority I hold seven stars [these are the angels of the seven churches]."

## YOUR GOOD POINTS

"I've seen all the good things you do. I know how hard you work and that you never give up. I know that you have no time for evil people. You have uncovered those people who pretend to be apostles."

*"Let anyone who has an ear listen to what the Spirit is saying to the churches."*

*Revelation 2:7*

## YOUR BAD POINTS

"But I do have some things against you. You don't love as strongly as you did at the beginning. So love as strongly as you used to. Start showing that love to other people. Anyone who has an ear, listen to what the Spirit is saying."

314

# The church in Smyrna

### THE FIRST AND THE LAST

This is the message to you who belong to the church in Smyrna: The One who is giving you this message is called the First and the Last. The One who is speaking to you is the One who was dead but is now alive again."

*"These are the words of
the first and the last,
who was dead and
came to life."*

Revelation 2:8

## SUFFERING

"I have nothing but good things to say to you about your strong faith in God. You're doing very well indeed. I know all about your troubles. You don't have a lot of money, but in faith terms you're millionaires. I know about those who are against you and about those untrue things they accuse you of. I'm afraid that you are going to suffer. In fact, some of you will be thrown into prison just because you are faithful followers of Jesus."

## MARTYRS

"Your suffering won't go on forever. You may be imprisoned, but even if you are killed, you are to remain faithful to God. God will reward you in heaven with the crown of life."

# The church in Pergamum

316

"This is the message to the church in Pergamum: The One who is speaking to you has a long two-edged sword in my hand which I use as I judge people."

*These are the words of one who has the sharp two-edged sword.*

*Revelation 2:12*

WELL DONE

"I know all about the tough place where you live, which is like living in Satan's city where Satan sits on the throne. But you have not given in and have remained true to me. Even when one Christian became a martyr, you still spoke out bravely about your faith in me. Very well done."

## YOU COULD DO BETTER

"But I do have a few things against you. There are some of you who follow evil teaching. This false teaching is like the teaching of Balaam, who led people away from God. You've got to put a stop to following this kind of teaching."

## YOUR REWARD

"You will have great rewards if you do stay faithful to me. In heaven you will feed on special food, like the manna God's people ate in the desert. You will also be given a white stone. On the white stone is written a secret name. This stone will be your ticket into heaven. Only you will know what name is on the stone. It will be your own name."

# The church in Laodicea

318

"This is the message to the seventh church in Asia, the church in Laodicea: The One giving you this message is called "Amen," as I am full of truth. I am a faithful and true witness. I rule over everything that God has made."

## LUKEWARM

"I have to tell you off for some of your serious faults. You are just like the pathetic water supply in the town of Laodicea which dries up so often. You are not hot or cold. Your love for me is wishy-washy; it's not one thing or the other. I'm going to spit you out of my mouth like disgusting tepid, lukewarm water.

"You swagger around town boasting about how rich you are. Because you have money you think that's all you need. But when it comes to serving God and loving God, you are at the bottom of the league. You are like a poor blind person who has to beg for food and clothes."

## BUY GOLD

"This must be your plan of action: buy gold from me. This gold will have been purified by fire. Then you will be rich in the spirit. Buy special clothes. Then you will be forgiven. Buy special medicine to cure your blindness, then you will see things as God sees them." Of course, the writer didn't mean that Christians should literally go shopping. Rather they needed to say they were sorry and to start living in God's way.

## KNOCKING ON THE DOOR

"And, remember, I'm only correcting you, because I love you so much. Change your lives. Change your hearts. I'm standing outside the door of your life. I'm knocking on the door. As you hear my voice, open up to me. Then I promise to come in, and I will sit down and have a good meal with you."

*"I know your works; you are neither cold nor hot."*

*Revelation 3:15*

*Revelation chapter 21 verses 1 to 6, and chapter 22 verses 1 to 5*

# New heaven and earth

320

The writer of Revelation imagined a time when troubles and persecution would end. Everything would be different.

"I see a new heaven and a new earth. The old heaven and earth have gone, and so has the sea of trouble. God is living right beside us. God will wipe away our tears. There will be no more pain or crying.

"A river, clear as crystal, will flow through our city. The tree of life will grow on its banks, bearing fruit not just once a year but every month, so no one will ever be hungry. What's more, this tree has leaves that heal every hurt.

"The throne of God and the Lamb (Jesus) will be there. God's servants will see God face to face. God's name will be written on their foreheads."

*On either side of the river is the tree of life.*

Revelation 22:2